THE FOURTEENTH OF JULY

PROFILES IN HISTORY

....

THE FOURTEENTH OF JULY

CHRISTOPHER PRENDERGAST

P
PROFILE BOOKS

First published in Great Britain in 2008 by
Profile Books Ltd
3A Exmouth House
Pine Street
Exmouth Market
London EC1R 0JH
www.profilebooks.com

1 3 5 7 9 10 8 6 4 2

Typeset in Palatino by MacGuru Ltd
info@macguru.org.uk
Printed and bound in Great Britain by
Clays, Bungay, Suffolk

A CIP catalogue record for this book is available from the British Library.

ISBN 978 1 86197 939 1

The paper this book is printed on is certified by the © 1996 Forest Stewardship
Council A.C. (FSC). It is ancient-forest friendly. The printer holds FSC chain of
custody SGS-COC-2061

FSC
Mixed Sources
Product group from well-managed
forests and other controlled sources

Cert no. SGS-COC-2061
www.fsc.org
© 1996 Forest Stewardship Council

For Clea

'Nothing'

Louis XVI's diary, 14 July 1789

'How much the greatest event it is that ever happened in the world. And how much the best'

Charles James Fox

'But, to the living and the struggling, a new, Fourteenth morning dawns. Under all roofs of this distracted City is the nodus of a drama, not untragical, crowding towards solution. The bustlings and preparings, the tremors and menaces; the tears that fell from old eyes! This day, my sons, ye shall quit you like men. By the memory of your fathers' wrongs, by the hope of your children's right! Tyranny impends in red wrath: help for you is none, if not in your own right hands. This day ye must do or die'

Thomas Carlyle, *The French Revolution*

CONTENTS

Part One: Events

1. Humbert's Day   3
2. The Revolutionary *journée*   17
3. The Convocation of the Estates-General   39
4. *A la Bastille!*   63

Part Two: Memory

5. The *Fête de la Fédération*   97
6. Bastille Day   127
7. The Centennial and the Bicentennial   159

   Further Reading   189
   List of Illustrations   195
   Acknowledgements   197
   Index   199

PART ONE: EVENTS

1. *After the event, the insurgents were officially designated 'Vainqueurs de la Bastille'. Thevenin's picture of an unnamed participant is a visual translation of reality into heroic legend, in pose and demeanour looking every inch the romantic-martial figure that was to be come the stock in trade of paintings of the young Napoleon Bonaparte. None of the insurgents was actually dressed like this on the day.*

1

HUMBERT'S DAY

'Where were you on the day that ... JFK was shot, the Berlin Wall came down, the Twin Towers were hit ...?' is a popular dinner-table game, or the kind of question with which the inquisitive young invite the knowledgeable old to reminisce. How many times the children and grandchildren of those who stormed the Bastille prison on 14 July 1789, and lived to tell the tale, were so regaled has to be anybody's guess. Many of the insurgents survived into a ripe old age, and it is not at all difficult to imagine them recollecting their adventure at the centre of a hushed and awestruck family circle. Someone who imagined them in roughly this way was Jules Michelet, the historian of the French Revolution who more than any other saw himself as the custodian of revolutionary memory. In the chapter on the Bastille episode in his *Histoire de la Révolution française* he attempts to resurrect the past (the moment of the storming itself) as if it were a living present, but also to project a future point of retrospect from which the original besiegers, now old ('vieillards'), speak of and to the meaning of their experience. Yet Michelet does not individualise his ageing *Vainqueurs de la Bastille* (or Heroes of the Bastille, as they came to be known); no one is named or quoted, we hear no personal voices. The imagined voice is entirely collective, a rhetorical device designed to carry a particular message: of all the major historical events the old men could have known in the space of their lifetimes, only 14 July 1789 'was the day of the whole people'. This distinction was to become part of the ongoing myth of that day's famous events.

Let us make our own first port of call one of these individual voices. It belongs to Jean-Baptiste Humbert, though not as an old man reminiscing to the young, but as the author of a tiny footnote in the vast revolutionary archive, the eyewitness account of the insurrection he wrote some time in the first half of August 1789, apparently at the request of the newly constituted Paris municipality: *Journée de Jean-Baptiste Humbert, horloger, Qui, le premier, a monté sur les Tours de la Bastille* (The day of Jean-Baptiste Humbert, Watchmaker, Who was the First to have Mounted the Bastille towers). It falls into two parts: a brief prefatory declaration of identity and intention to an assumed readership addressed as 'Frenchmen, my compatriots', followed by the longer narrative account of the 'day' itself. Our knowledge of Humbert derives entirely from this document. In it he tells us that he was a native of Langres in the department of Haute-Marne, and that as of 1787 he was an artisan employed in Paris by the royal watchmaker, Belliard, in the rue du Hurepoix (the street which coincidentally housed the publisher and bookstore Gueffier, which printed the French translation of Thomas Paine's *Common Sense*). He also tells us that he spent some time as a journeyman apprentice in Geneva and was there at the time of the 1782 rebellion demanding equality of political rights and its suppression by the Genevan 'patrician' oligarchy with French military assistance.

Beyond these autobiographical facts, we know nothing of his background, especially how and where he would have acquired the relevant literacy skills to compose his account. Most of the eyewitness reports of 14 July were written by often highly educated journalists and municipal representatives. Humbert was not one of these. His account has a refreshing 'simplicity' in the best sense of the term, unclogged by the kinds of heavy-handed sententiousness that sometimes characterise the more official depositions. As a lens through which to view, in however fragmentary and incomplete a form, the manner in which 14 July 1789 unfolded, Humbert's text is of value for three things. First, it provides a narrative of some of the main events of the day, and crucially – as we shall see in more detail later – the turning point at which the invasion of the prison became a siege properly speaking, the consequence of which was the surrender by the governor, Bernard de Launay; secondly, as an 'insider's' view, it gives some sense of the lived texture of those events, largely as a whirlwind of chance and muddle; thirdly – and perhaps its most interesting feature – in telling us of Humbert's motives, thoughts and feelings as a participant, the document reveals the extent to which it is the reflection of a particular subjectivity caught up in the maelstrom of history.

Humbert's story starts on the streets of Paris, specifically in the district of Saint-André-des-Arts (in the Latin Quarter). It is 12 July 1789. Unbeknownst to everyone and planned by no one, the French Revolution is about to 'begin', with the occurrence two days later of what retrospectively came to be identified as the inaugural event: the storming of the Bastille. What is widely known (presumably by Humbert too) is that insurrection is in the air. Negotiations between the king, Louis XVI, and the newly formed National Assembly over political and fiscal reform have broken down. Louis's finance minister, the popular Necker, has been dismissed. Troops have been dispatched to encircle the city. In part to meet this perceived threat, the Paris authorities have instigated the creation of a citizens' militia to defend the people. This is the context in which Humbert's personal story accedes to the stage of history-in-the-making.

On 12 July he gets news of a clash in the Tuileries gardens between a crowd of demonstrators and a detachment of troops under the command of the prince de Lambesc, the first major indication of imminent uprising. But the lines of conflict have already been blurred. For there is also 'news that the armed populace was attacking the Bourgeois instead of defending them', the term 'Bourgeois' here referring to the hastily constituted civilian militia (it was sometimes called the *milice bourgeoise*). Confusion and contradiction, against a background of mounting fear and violence, thus mark the point of Humbert's entry into the sequence of events that will lead to the storming of the Bastille. He appears to have offered his services to the Saint-André-des-Arts unit of the militia and to have spent most of his time on patrol from Monday 13 July throughout the day and the night into 14 July.

In discharging these civic duties, however, all he and his fellow militia have are 'swords', the 'District having no fire-arms or only a few'. On the morning of the 14th, 'overcome with weariness and lack of food and sleep', Humbert makes his way, with thousands of others, to the Invalides (the retirement home for aged and disabled veterans), 'where arms for the various Districts were being distributed' (in actual fact less a distribution than a seizure). Humbert arrives at the Invalides at around 2 p.m. All is sheer chaos. On the steps leading down to the cellars, where the weapons are stored, the press of bodies is such that some are crushed, many

faint and even more are 'shrieking and gasping for breath'.
Humbert is caught twice in the press, falling back down into
the cellar, but is 'only shaken and not injured by the fall'.
He grabs two muskets, gives one away, and together with
a number of other armed citizens manages to impose some
sort of crowd control. If, as is indeed the case, a revolution is
about to erupt, the ingredients of the revolutionary mix are
little short of a mess.

The acquired muskets are, however, useless without
ammunition and so, in search of powder and shot, Humbert
begins stage two of his revolutionary odyssey. This takes
him first to the Hôtel de Ville (the town hall), where he is
given 'a quarter pound of powder but no shot, saying they
had none' ('they' probably Jacques de Flesselles, the *prévôt
des marchands*, in charge of munitions at the town hall and
who was to pay with his life on the night of the 14th for his
alleged mendacity over the question of arms). As he leaves
the Hôtel de Ville, Humbert learns of another development
('I heard someone say that the Bastille was being besieged').
This is to become his principal destination, but not before a
number of Parisian detours hunting for the elusive and des-
perately needed ammunition. He has a bright idea. Why not
buy some nails from an ironmonger ('which I got from the
grocer's at the Coin du Roi at the place de Grève') and use
these as makeshift shot? On exiting from the grocer's shop,
he is 'accosted by a Citizen' who informs him that shot is
in fact being handed out at the Hôtel de Ville (a desperate
attempt by the municipal authorities to control the circulation of weapons). Humbert retraces his steps, is supplied
with 'half a dozen pellets of buckshot' and sets off for the
Bastille. En route he passes the Hôtel de la Régie (the excise
office), from which several cases of bullets had been raided.

Humbert is given enough to fill a coat pocket. Still further detours and adventures await him on his way to the Bastille, one of which we shall return to in another connection.

It is thus quite late by the time Humbert arrives at the prison (around 3.30). Much has of course already taken place; there are already many dead and wounded. But his arrival, and hence his story, coincides more or less with the arrival of both professional soldiers (defectors from the contingents of royal troops) and military hardware (cannon), led by Hulin and Elie (both of whom were to become adulated heroes of the siege). It was this development that broke Launay's will and secured a capitulation. Humbert is no mere bystander or observer at this decisive moment. He helps to wheel the cannon into position and on the approach to the drawbridge which leads to the inner citadel he finds himself 'in the front rank'. Stepping over two dead bodies, under a barrage of gunfire, he advances to the drawbridge, while the cannon is trained on the entrance to the inner courtyard. He assists with the laying of a plank across the moat, when a piece of paper with Launay's terms is passed through a gap in the entrance. One man crossing the plank to take the paper is hit by a bullet and, mortally wounded, falls into the moat. Launay's terms are rejected. The cannon is about to fire when the entrance gate is opened. The besiegers pour in, Humbert ahead of the pack, and he climbs – allegedly the first to do so – the steps of one of the prison towers, where he finds and disarms one of the contingent of Swiss Guards assigned to Launay to defend the Bastille (much of the royal army was made up of foreign mercenaries). Still on the tower, Humbert is trying to disable one of the enemy cannon when he receives a bullet in the neck, collapses senseless and is saved only by the ministrations of the Swiss Guard he has taken into custody. This is to produce a further, unexpected and ironically near-disastrous turn of events (to which we shall revert shortly), but in terms of the main drama Humbert's narrative and the history it reflects – the storming of the Bastille – are effectively over. Humbert has his wounds treated, sets off for home under armed guard (not without further mishap, which results in his taking refuge in the home of an acquaintance), rests up until midnight and then, ever indefatigable, rises from his sickbed to report to the commanding officer of the Saint-André-des-Arts militia for further duties ('under whose orders I remained until the following morning').

For Humbert himself, the main point of his summary was its veracity, the form of that insistence – as we shall see – of interest in its own right. But this is scarcely its main point for us. Stripped of its multiple contingencies, Humbert's story can indeed serve as a matrix, encapsulating some of the key reference points which the historian, looking back, uses to shape an intelligible narrative: the atmosphere of collective fear, the self-arming of the citizenry, the formation of the militia, the search for weapons in different parts of the city, the critical moment at which the Bastille fell. But to strip it in this way is to rob the tale of a great deal, above all its immediacy and subjective resonance, the feel it gives us of what it was like on the ground, in all its chaotic unpredictability. The disorder at the Invalides, the uncertainty on 12 July over who is attacking whom, who is friend and who is enemy, are already signs that here is an unfolding situation that, for those experiencing it, is in many ways the obverse of the readily intelligible.

And there is more, much more. Humbert is determined to enrol in the militia, but is unsure which district he belongs to

(Saint-André-des-Arts is merely a guess, probably because the militia is in the process of being constituted, such that no one quite knows how it is being organised). Furthermore, on his journey across Paris to the Bastille, like a proto-version of the good soldier Schweik, he is caught up in a fast-moving flow of random encounters and bizarre incidents. Perhaps the most startlingly unexpected is what happens at the Hôtel de la Régie. After retrieving the bullets, Humbert hears 'a woman calling for help'. He approaches and is informed that someone is setting fire to the saltpetre store, why unknown. In he goes, to find what appears to be a demented wigmaker 'holding a lighted torch in each hand, with which he was in fact setting fire to the place'. Humbert, with no time to enquire why a wigmaker might want to blow up a stock of saltpetre, knocks him over with the butt of his rifle, extinguishes the fire and, before continuing on his way, is asked to deal with another incident: to 'drive out certain ill-intentioned people who had forced their way in and broken into the documents room'.

But the high point of the genre of happenstance and pandemonium is what happens once inside the Bastille and after leaving it. The Swiss Guard who helps Humbert to his feet after he has been shot in the neck is mistaken by the crowd as the perpetrator of Humbert's wound ('seeing me covered in blood, they assumed that the Swiss must have wounded me, and tried to kill him'). Only after words of explanation is the Swiss spared. But there is to be a further twist in this saga of menace based on misapprehension, this time in respect of Humbert himself. On seeing him return home under armed escort after his wound has been treated, the crowd assumes that he has been taken captive and prepares to administer summary revolutionary justice ('we were followed by a crowd of people who mistook me for a malefactor, and twice attempted to put me to death'). Only with the intervention of a bookseller who recognises him and takes him to safety is the danger averted. As we shall see, cases of mistaken identity and misinterpreted actions were par for the course on 14 July, of a kind that blurs the historical canvas and confounds the historian's characteristic wish for a 'cleanly' delineated narrative.

Finally, there is the question of what impelled Humbert to take part, what he felt, desired, imagined and, relatedly, what it meant for him to write his account a few weeks later. The striking feature is a certain sharpness of political consciousness. All the buzzwords are there: liberty, patriots, citizens, etc. We are in no position to determine independently whether these are load-bearing terms, in the sense of reflecting what actually went through Humbert's mind at the time of joining the insurrection, or alternatively whether they are afterthoughts expressed in a language instantly and massively put into circulation in the interval between 14 July and the moment of writing in early August. Take, for example, Humbert's reference to his time in Geneva ('where I was working as a journeyman when that Republic lost its liberty'). This already weaves together autobiography and political history. In addition, speaking as someone who has already seen an uprising and has a view on what it meant, Humbert makes a specific allusion to the Genevan episode that has some direct bearing on 14 July and its immediate aftermath:

I witnessed the dismay of the townspeople, and I heard the curses they uttered against a certain Minister of France, who, they said, had deceived my King; I heard so many sighs, complaints and regrets, that for a long time I

bore in my heart something of the same feeling towards
that Minister as the unfortunate people of Geneva.

The minister is almost certainly Charles Gravier de Vergennes, in charge of foreign affairs under Louis XVI, who had
endorsed France's support of the American Revolution, not
from radical sympathies but because he judged it to be in the
national interest, exactly the consideration which governed
his support for French involvement in counter-revolutionary measures in Geneva. Humbert's distinction between a
deceived king and a manipulative minister raises the question
as to whether his were the already formed views of a politically self-conscious individual, such that they go a long way
in explaining his motives for participating in the events of 14
July; or were picked up immediately afterwards as post-facto
rationalisations. For, in connection with the events leading up
to the fall of the Bastille, the theme of the good king led astray
by his ministerial entourage was a commonplace of many of
the other eyewitness accounts, and conforms with the political settlement that the leaders wanted, a settlement in the
form of a constitutional monarchy, which they believed had
been amicably achieved on 15 July, when the king went before
the National Assembly, and on 17 July, when he presented
himself to the Paris municipality and the National Guard.
In other words, was the implied analogy between Geneva
1782 and France 1789 already part of Humbert's world view,
inspiring his sense of what, on the day itself, 14 July was fundamentally about? Or did it come to him only later, when,
as he sat down to write in the following weeks, the belief
in an innocent and well-meaning monarch was already the
new orthodoxy, a belief encouraged by those in charge of the
propaganda machine and given wide publicity in press and

pamphlet? In his account is he expressing long-held convictions or subsequently acquired ones, even perhaps merely repeating what he knows others would like to hear?

There is no way this question of before or after can be satisfactorily resolved, since we have no further sources of information about Humbert on which to draw. Yet everything about the tone of his report suggests someone whose attitudes and beliefs were formed well before the patriotic slogans were to be found on everybody's lips, and they may well have been forged in his Genevan experience. Here is a man who volunteers spontaneously for the militia, who positively seeks it out while uncertain as to which unit he belongs. Even more telling is his behaviour throughout the day of 14 July. He is running from pillar to post, and at every single point of his itinerary he responds to calls for, or actively offers help. At the Invalides he gives away one of the two guns he has seized. He assists with bringing out the victims of the crush on the cellar steps. On his way to the Bastille he encounters four soldiers of the watch and shares his ammunition with them. At the Hôtel de la Régie he stuffs his pocket with bullets 'to give to anyone who was short'. He answers the woman's call for help in connection with the saltpetre episode. He acts when the 'household staff came to beg me to help them' with the 'ill-intentioned people' who had burst into the documents room. Once inside the Bastille, 'I rushed over to the staircase to help the citizens, whom I assumed to have been driven back'. He helps to save the Swiss Guard from otherwise certain death.

The word 'help' appears on virtually every page, but nowhere is it ostentatiously paraded as illustrating the virtues of the revolutionary Patriot. On each occasion, it is merely noted, as if in passing, as just one detail among

others registered as he bumps into whatever and whom-
ever happen to cross his path. The low-key manner makes
it tempting to read this as merely expressing the common
decencies of the ordinary man. But there is just too much of
this sort of thing to sustain that banal interpretation. It's as if
a code of civic duty has been fully internalised, as the living
demonstration of a consciously assumed ethic of solidarity
in the midst of a political crisis; in its understated way, it
is tantamount to being the declaration of a creed, close in
spirit to what the eighteenth-century political thinkers had
defined as the republic of virtue.

There is also the question of what for Humbert were the
purpose and meaning of writing down his account. At one
level he seems to be in the world evoked by Michelet or the
world of where-were-you-on-the-day-that ... He tells us how
happy he is 'to have given some pleasure to my relatives by
the story of my actions'. But he also adds: 'I do not want
the town of Langres to give any credence to the information
given by my relatives until I have the signatures of all those
whom I have mentioned in my statement'. These are the signatures of the 'gentlemen of the Hôtel de Ville'. It amounts
to something of an obsession; he wants not just some but
all the signatures of those who can attest the truthfulness of
his account ('They were witnesses to everything that I have
alleged, and so I need the signatures of all these witnesses').

And so it is that the published text carries a postscript
signed by some of the other insurgents: Ducastel, Maillard, Richard, Dupin and Georget. There may have been
an element of self-interest in this demand, confirmation of
Humbert's claim that he was the 'first' to scale the Bastille
towers (many other witnesses were to have recourse to the
same tactic, often to secure a false claim to fame). But what is

clear is that Humbert was offering not just personal reminis-
cences for a limited family circle ('relatives'), but a record for
posterity. He is anxious for private recollections to become,
through validation by others, authenticated public testimony.
In the later course of the Revolution a quite different politics
of testimony was to emerge. With the onset of the Terror, the
revolutionary surveillance committees had a standard question for 'suspects', in its general form not entirely dissimi-
lar to the notorious *question* asked by the Bastille authorities
(the euphemistic word for an interrogation often accompanied by torture): *Où étois-tu le 14 juillet*? ('Where were you on
14 July?'). In this context, 'memory' was subordinate to ruse,
since the answer given could be a matter of life and death,
with independent verification often crucial to whether or not
the suspect was believed.

Humbert of course could not have had anything like
this in mind. The 'days' of the great *sans-culotte* insurrections were some years off. But one thing that his text has
in common with that later discourse is lexical: the main
term of his title, *Journée de Jean-Baptiste Humbert*. It is almost
certain that Humbert intended the word *journée* in the sense
in which it is normally understood: a 'day', specifically *his*
day, a day-in-the-life-of, albeit of an unusually charged kind.
But it was not long before it came to acquire a new meaning
for the revolutionary actors themselves, one that was retrospectively applied to the events of 14 July. While we should
therefore beware of anachronism, it is nevertheless hard to
resist hearing in Humbert's invocation of his 'day' something of that meaning to come. Its precise content, along
with its application to what took place on 14 July 1789, is the
subject of the next chapter, as one of the framing contexts for
understanding the events themselves.

2. *With the Bastille fortress looming in the background and attacking cannon in the foreground, Lallemand's picture represents the turning point of the siege of the storming of 14 July (the moment when the defecting* gardes françaises *arrived in mid-afternoon with artillery). The painting transforms what was a ragged and improvised attack into the register of epic.*

2

THE REVOLUTIONARY *JOURNÉE*

The weather, if not always propitious to the French Revolution itself, has often been a godsend to its many romancers and fabulators. On the first anniversary of the taking of the Bastille, the grandly organised spectacle on the Champ de Mars (the *Fête de la Fédération*) was washed out by torrential rain – an incontrovertible sign to those of pessimistic and ironic dispositions that the Revolution was all a terrible mistake. On the second anniversary, however, the weather was glorious, suggesting to those of sunnier temperaments that, despite the political evidence to the contrary, all was for the best in the best of all possible worlds. For the *Fête de l'Etre Suprême* in 1794, the rhyming of Robespierre's famously immaculate sky-blue coat with the cerulean aspect of the heavens seemed like a godsend expressly dispatched by the Supreme Being himself, prompting one of Robespierre's less felicitous equations of benign nature and revolutionary politics: 'Nature, how sublime, how delightful thy power! How the tyrants must turn pale at the thought of this Festival' (they were more likely to turn pale at the thought of the guillotine, which for the duration of the festival had been discreetly moved from view to – of all places – the site of the now demolished Bastille).

But by far the most telling alignment of weather and

history comes on the day subsequently dedicated by the French state to commemoration in perpetuity, the day of the actual taking of the Bastille: 14 July 1789. At daybreak, according to Michelet, the sky was 'luminous'. By late morning, as armed crowds swarmed through the streets of the capital, black clouds gathered, threatening a violent summer storm. By late afternoon the city found itself bathed in warm and mellow sunshine; in the course of a few hours, a massive turbulence had been followed by sweetness and light. To the great poet-historians of the Revolution these were irresistible coincidences, as if the physical atmosphere had spontaneously moulded itself to its political counterpart. The equations were, however, flexible, depending on ideological preferences. Carlyle's late-afternoon sunshine has a distinctly bloodshot garishness to it, held to illuminate 'one general wreck of madness', while by 22 July, with all apparently settled and reconciled, 'there is halcyon weather; weather even of preternatural brightness; the hurricane being overblown'.

Days of this world-historical calibre are rare and it is thus unsurprising that writers invest them with all manner of inflated literary currency. The customary historical units for this kind of treatment are the century and the millennium, most notably attracting the convenient shaping fictions of beginning and ending, with a strong emphasis on the latter, the end as the arrival of end-time. But, if these are the standard units, there are others, including the decade, the year and the day (and, on occasion, the night: *Kristallnacht*). The day is something we more typically associate with the rhythms of everyday life, as the measure of humdrum personal time. Days are quite simply, as Philip Larkin's poem has it, 'where we live'. They go largely unnoticed, apart from certain ritual punctuations of the continuum marked by important occasions in the skein of private and family life (birthdays, for example). These are the moments when the routines of the day are interrupted in favour of a Day, a special object of commemoration, celebratory in the matter of birth, doleful in the remembrance of a death.

This translation is not, however, unique to private life. In certain circumstances, the day can become a Day that possesses high public significance. The latter comes in all shapes and sizes. There is the singular day and the cluster of days (The Ten Days That Shook the World, *les trois glorieuses*). Streets have been named after some of them (the rue du 4 septembre). Some mark customs of national life (the Queen's Birthday). Some are reminders of catastrophic events: Holocaust Day; or 9/11, a number at once singular (a precise date in September 2001) and abstract, its indeterminate reference as pure number nevertheless laden with sorrowful meaning. Some have proved movable (the Ivory Coast became fully independent on 7 August 1960, but Independence Day has since moved to 7 December). Some are simply perverse: Anzac Day in Australia celebrates a military defeat, the irony of which is caught by an Australian acquaintance of mine who every year phones the Turkish Embassy to congratulate them on a victory. And then there is the kind represented by Bastille Day.

To belong to this kind, several conditions need to be satisfied. First, the commemorating Day has to occur on the same date as the commemorated event; fixity appears to be an index of seriousness, whereas mobility seems to grant priority to convenience over solemnity. Secondly, its remembrance must be institutionalised, part of the official fabric of public life, or what the French call a *lieu de mémoire*. Thirdly, it must possess a certain durability, sustained by a consensus of sorts, even when eventually frayed at the edges or subjected to forms of amnesia or indifference. Fourthly – and most importantly – it has to mark a certain kind of event: namely, what is held to be a founding moment, an experience of historical rupture that is perceived as an absolute beginning. Its commanding tropes are 'Dawn', 'Birth' and 'Resurrection'. This condition necessarily excludes days of catastrophe remembrance, conducted as lamentation or in silence, by definition not days of public celebration.

In the political calendar of Western modernity, there are two cases which most fully satisfy all four of these conditions: 4 July 1776 in the United States and 14 July 1789 in France, both posited as founding moments of what in each case was to be declared a republic (and, relatedly, 'democracy'). What they share is a reputation comparable to no other, in the affirmative register of events deemed in retrospect to be shattering breaks, initiating something radically and irreversibly new, with rippling consequences for substantial portions of mankind. What they also share are serious mismatches between myth and reality, a gap between the imagined and the true in which 'collective memory' does its shaping work. There is an important sense in which collective memory is not memory at all, but rather the fashioning of a story that a community (national, ethnic, religious) likes to tell about its past both to itself and to others. The relation of that story to what actually took place is often skewed.

But if this is what the Fourth of July and the Fourteenth of July have in common, there are also substantial differences, both narrative and symbolic, although we should avoid the temptation – many have conspicuously failed – of using these in the fatuous game of assessing which of the two, the American or the French, was the 'better' revolution. Far preferable is the alleged response of the Chinese leader Zhou Enlai to the question of the historical impact of the French Revolution: 'too early to tell'. The differences, however, are real and the contrastive picture provides a useful way of focusing on both what was distinctive about 14 July 1789 and the ways in which it has been subsequently remembered. The principal differences are threefold. The first concerns variations in historical and political context. The Declaration of Independence expressed, or more exactly performed, the rejection by the American colonists of rule from afar, specifically the authority of the king, George III, though, as subjects under the crown whose right to the colonies was secured by royal warrant, they were not explicitly anti-monarchical as such. Neither of these considerations applies to 14 July. The issues surrounding the Parisian uprising were entirely internal to the nation. And although there was much mistrust of Louis XVI's intentions, no one, at least at this stage, apart from a few firebrands, conceived the project of an end to monarchy. In so far as 14 July was animated by any clear political aspirations at all, the aim was to temper not liquidate royal authority, by replacing absolutism based on the doctrine of divine right with a constitutional arrangement under which the monarch ceded a large measure of sovereignty to a national assembly of representatives.

The second major difference concerns the terms on which the respective Days have been commemorated. There have been attempts to link them. Two of the besiegers of the Bastille were soldiers who had fought in the War of Independence, while the most illustrious French combatant in the American war, Lafayette, was later to present George Washington with the keys to the Bastille. Yet this produced no enduring commemorative kinship. In France 14 July became an occasion of state, and remains such. In the United States, although most presidents make a speech somewhere, 4 July is not an official state ceremony. There is good reason why it is not, connected to the long history of federalism and anti-federalism that informed both the founding and the making of the United States. The words 'federalism' and 'anti-federalism' were understood quite differently in France, and where points of contact between the two commemorations concerned. This has often lead to curious, and confused, affiliations. For instance, in the United States it was the anti-federalists in Boston and Philadelphia who incorporated the fall of the Bastille and the tricolour flag into their own 4 July festivities. But this reflected a misunderstanding: in France it was the 'federalists' (keen on regional autonomy) who approximated most closely to what in the United States went under the banner of anti-federalism (states' rights), while the main thrust of the anti-federalist cause in France pulled in the opposite direction, towards an ever more centralised state. In short, across the divide of the Atlantic, we encounter, around a roughly common vocabulary, very different political conceptions reacting to and informing very different circumstances.

It is, however, the third difference that is the most striking of all, in the character of the events themselves that took place. In the case of 4 July, there is from the word go a disjunct between what actually occurred (or rather what did *not* occur) and the celebratory fiction. Every American schoolchild is taught that the document which is now preserved in an airless box in Washington (the transcript to velum of the printed broadsheet circulating the revised version of Jefferson's draft declaration) was signed by the overwhelming majority of the Founders. It was indeed, but it was not signed in Philadelphia on 4 July (at which time most of the Founders were absent elsewhere on business; both the transcription and the collective signing came some time later). What, if anything, was signed and by whom on 4 July are matters that remain obscure (if there was a signed document, it was probably an unfinished draft of some sort, but, if so, there were probably only two signatories, John Hancock and another). By contrast, there is no doubt whatsoever that something both determinate and dramatic took place in Paris on 14 July. The latter had its own raggedness, but it was far more cohesive *as a day* on which something definitive and defining took place: the Bastille was taken, an event in itself, as Georges Lefebvre put it, 'of minor importance' but momentous in consequence.

Furthermore, while the Declaration of Independence is normally described as a 'revolutionary' act, what happened in Philadelphia on 4 July – albeit against the background of an ongoing war of independence – was entirely peaceable, taken up with meetings, speeches, texts and, maybe, signatures. Its rough equivalent in France might be the National Assembly debating in Versailles, especially its self-declaration *as* a national assembly on 17 June 1789, consolidated three days later by the famous Tennis Court Oath. This was a harbinger of things to come, and the French Revolution would soon be awash in speeches, texts and signatures. But the modality of the events of 14 July was the brandishing not of bits of paper but of guns and pikes. It was an armed insurrection, an action on the streets backed by force of arms and as such entirely illegal. While we must be alert to the traps of reading 'backwards' from the perspective of subsequent developments, especially given the huge differences of both scale and intensity, 14 July is often seen as a dress rehearsal for the great *sans-culotte* uprisings of the period 1792–5 (although the view that 'the Terror was merely 1789 with a higher body count' is closer to headline-seeking journalism than to responsible historical enquiry). The Declaration of Independence, though of course illegal from the point of view of the king and his ministers, was intended as a legal document, outlining why George III had abdicated his rights over the colonists. The latter were well versed in the legal literature and were essentially saying that, as in 1688, the king had acted 'illegally' in respect of his subjects. But 14 July was not like this at all. No lawyerly arguments were made by those who stormed the Bastille. It was a day of violence, of a type which was to yield a new meaning for the word 'day' itself: what the historical actors were shortly to call the revolutionary *journée*, by now indicating a great deal more than was intended by its appearance in the title of Jean-Baptiste Humbert's account.

The *journée* was not merely a sum of time. Nor was it just a significant date, of which, in the French Revolution, there are so many as to be almost too numerous to mention. For the year 1789 alone, claimants in this category for the prize of the most significant would include 5 May (the meeting of the Estates-General), 20 June (the Tennis Court Oath), 4 August (the official end to 'feudal' privilege) and 26 August (the Declaration of the Rights of Man and the Citizen). Indeed, if it were simply a matter of dates, the key example would have be the ground-clearing reinvention of dates itself, the Republican calendar promulgated by decree of the National Convention in November 1793 to replace the gregorian calendar and which, as a political artefact, backdated the new order of time whereby 22 September 1792 notionally became

Day 1 of Year 1. In fact, 21 September was the date on which the monarchy officially ended, and – if somewhat squeamishly (the term was smuggled into a revised declaration published the following day) – the Republic came into being on 22 September. If a given point is to serve as foundational, the marker of a new 'beginning', this has to be it. But a calendrical date is not at all the same thing as a revolutionary *journée*. For a day to be classified as a *journée*, it was not enough for it to be deemed historically momentous; it had to involve degrees of unrest, turbulence, menace and, generally if not always, riot and repression; crucially, it had to involve the actions of the common people. The womens' march on Versailles in October 1789, the Champ de Mars Massacre of 17 July 1791, the invasions of the Tuileries palace on 20 June and 10 August 1792, the September Massacres of 1792, the siege of the Convention on 2 June 1793, the *sans-culotte* insurgencies of 1–2 April and 20–23 May 1795 – these are some of the more memorable *journées* which have taken up permanent residence in the history books.

But, in a field crowded with rivals, it is 14 July 1789 which remains the most memorable of them all, as the only one that has survived in the wider consciousness and the only one to receive the imprimatur of a national festival and a public holiday. If in the Republican calendar 22 September 1792 is the beginning of Year 1 of the Republic, 14 July 1789 is the beginning of what was to be called Year 1 of Liberty. It has, however, acquired this status at the cost of a certain process of 'forgetting' what the day was fundamentally about. For us it is very difficult to access the thoughts, motives and emotions of those who took part in the storming of the Bastille. Even those who in the immediate aftermath committed their own version of events to print are not necessarily reliable guides to what actually went through their minds on the day itself. The storming was not on the whole a collectively focused or cogently led enterprise. But neither was it random 'mob' violence, the anarchic behaviour of the 'swinish multitude', in Edmund Burke's trope subsequently much favoured by right-wing historians. However inarticulate and inchoate, there was a real sense of purpose, albeit reactive rather than proactive.

The call to arms was not to overthrow the state (a ludicrous ambition), but a call to self-defence. It is true that by day's end on the 14th there was already talk of having toppled a symbol of 'despotism' (success breeds its own meanings), but at the beginning of the day the main concerns had less to do with symbolism than with practicality. The crowd that swept across Paris from the place de Grève, the faubourg Saint-Antoine and the Invalides to the Bastille had no plan to destroy a physical structure (the Bastille was, if not impregnable, indestructible), nor was it propelled by a desire to 'liberate' the prison's inmates (such as they were, seven in all, including two madmen and four forgers). It rallied to the cry *à la Bastille!* as a gigantic raiding party intent on seizing an eminently useful commodity: gunpowder (large amounts of which had been removed to the Bastille for safekeeping). For over two weeks the city had been ringed by an estimated 25,000 royal troops. We do not know whether this was on the direct orders of Louis XVI or stipulated by his ministers. Nor do we know what the precise motive was: whether as a policing operation to maintain public order, a gesture of intimidation or a prelude to an actual military repression (most of the evidence suggests the strategy was defensive rather than offensive). Nevertheless, it was seen by the people of Paris as a real threat to both itself and the National Assembly in

Versailles. The eruption took place less from anger at unacknowledged grievances and unsatisfied demands than from fear of assault.

It was, however, also a *journée* – this is what makes it authentically revolutionary – in the sense that its violence addressed or precipitated a crisis of authority around the question who rules France? The question was provisionally resolved the following day. On the 15th the king went in person to the fledgling National Assembly to concede a shift of sovereignty from absolutism to the 'nation', the National Assembly itself converting to a Constituent Assembly charged with the task of designing a constitution binding on all, and in theory based on the promulgation in late August of the Declaration of the Rights of Man and the Citizen. But if 15 July is about the formal delivery of outcomes (the promise of a new constitutional dispensation and a new form of political legitimacy), 14 July has nothing to do with either the constitutional or the legitimate. On the 14th the question who rules received the answer: on this day no one rules, or the 'people' rules, and it does so not through some representative institution safeguarding and in turn safeguarded by a set of laws, but from the streets. It is a *journée* by virtue of being a day on which legal authority ceased to exist as a practical proposition.

Article 11 of the Declaration included the right of 'resistance to oppression'. The inclusion was intended in part as the retroactive conferral of legal sanction by the Assembly on the uprising of 14 July. But in respect of the 14th itself, the National Assembly was a non-player. It sat in Versailles wringing its hands, debating this and that, sending out deputations and delegations, but was essentially powerless to act (the lines of communication with Paris were broken on the

13th as a consequence of the Sèvres and Saint-Cloud bridges having been placed under military guard). The king of course had the army. Yet, despite some skirmishes, the royal troops encircling the city were not ordered to attack. In fact it can be argued that the real meaning of the fall of the Bastille was not the capitulation of the prison, but that the army was not used to prevent it. In the event, their commander, Besenval, ordered a pull-back to the Champ de Mars, probably because he had not received any clear orders, but also perhaps because the evidence of desertion to the side of the insurgents convinced him that, while enjoying overwhelmingly superior numbers, he could not guarantee their loyalty to the crown. But whatever the reasons, the retreat was effectively to forfeit what some have seen as the very definition of the state: monopoly over the legitimate use of violence.

Finally, there was also the improvised municipal body that was to base itself permanently in the Hôtel de Ville and to take the name of the Paris Commune. Its members – drawn from the Parisian Electors to the Estates-General – understood immediately the importance of force, creating in great haste the civilian militia later baptised as the National Guard under the command of Lafayette. One of its purposes was to organise resistance to the king's troops in the event of an attack. But another – as Humbert's report suggests – was to control the rioters and maintain public order in the face of incipient 'anarchy', a particular source of concern (shared by a large section of the civil population) being the number of vagabonds, convicts (liberated from other prisons) and further uncontrollable 'elements' in circulation on the streets. The bulk of the militia did not see it this way and sided with the 'people'. In the meantime, the Electors tried to assert whatever authority they had assumed by acting as an intermediary body that would negotiate a peaceful solution with Launay, the governor of the Bastille. All their initiatives failed. Indeed, the Hôtel de Ville itself was seriously menaced by the crowd in the immediate aftermath of the fall of the Bastille, on suspicion of harbouring 'traitors' (one of the members of its permanent committee, Jacques de Flesselles, was dragged from the building and shot).

In short, on three fronts – monarchy, assembly, municipality – constituted and self-constituting authority was broken, relinquished or simply non-existent. In this respect 14 July remains the exemplary *journée* by virtue of being the first in a series which laid bare a power vacuum, the attempted occupancy of which defines the 'logic' of the Revolution as a whole. No one grasped this logic more clearly, and more chillingly, than Robespierre. His principal argument concerned the relation between ends and means, based on the view that the Revolution was a transitional zone, a passage from a corrupt political order to the virtuous republic. The transition entailed the separation of 'justice' from law. Since present laws are merely entrenched injustice, the creation of the just society necessarily involves bypassing them. On the overthrow of the monarchy on 10 August 1792 he observed: 'The Revolution is illegal: the fall of the Bastille and of the monarchy were illegal – as illegal as liberty itself.' At the trial of Louis XVI he stated that 'a deposed king in the midst of a revolution as yet unsupported by just laws' cannot enjoy the customary protections of due process, adding that 'a people does not judge as a court of law'. This was a constant of Robespierre's thought, and it can be detected as early as the events surrounding the fall of the Bastille. The lynching of Foulon, the king's minister, in the days following elicited the comment: 'M. Foulon was hanged yesterday by the people's decree.'

Whatever Robespierre's opinions (and our opinion of those opinions), the fact remains that his analysis was unerringly accurate, one moreover shared by figures on the right, although from a very different political perspective (Thomas Carlyle represented Foulon's death as the exercise of 'wild justice'). The French Revolution, especially on its great *journées*, was fundamentally about the suspension of legality, the pressing of a cause by violent means, and the attempted annexation of an 'empty' space of power from which nearly all traditional sources of legitimacy had drained away. For better or for worse, this is what revolutions are. And if, because of his own willingness to go to the limit in the bloodstained chapter of the Terror, we find Robespierre's pitilessly lucid account too inhumanly cold, we can always turn to the more gentlemanly tones of the king's adviser, the duc de Liancourt, whispering into Louis's ear during the night of 14 July: 'No Sire, this is not a rebellion, it is a revolution.' Liancourt was also to state that it is 'very difficult to enter the domain of true liberty through such a door'. Robespierre thought otherwise, and came to grief. In a very different political idiom, Lafayette also thought it was possible, and to do so in such a way that the Revolution could be rendered 'legal'. His own recipe for this reconciled state of affairs came out of the events of 14 July: a monarchy both constrained by a constitution and secured by a monopoly on the use of violence vested in a National Guard commanded by himself. Many of the participants in the storming of the Bastille shared that belief. But in this Lafayette was also to prove hopelessly detached from reality, as the Revolution ran its course in ways he either failed to predict or deeply feared.

Eric Hobsbawm has written in *The Age of Revolution* that 'the capture of the Bastille' has 'rightly made 14 July into the French national day'. Among historians he is part of a large company that, notwithstanding variations of method, style and emphasis, runs from Michelet's *Histoire de la Révolution française* down through the nineteenth century to the present. On the other hand, by no means do all the historians of the French Revolution share this view. Many would take issue with the self-assurance of the adverb 'rightly', from a set of historiographical and political alignments closer in spirit to the conservative tradition opened by Burke's *Reflections on the French Revolution* (among the French historians of today, Pierre Chaunu is the most vitriolic partisan of this school of thought, for whom even the revolutionary abolition of the Church tithe was an abomination). The question has always been what 14 July 1789 is to be remembered *for*, and the answers given have always reflected different interests, preferences and agendas. 'Memory', in this context, has always been less about remembering a past than about interpreting its 'legacy'. To some extent this reflects sheer manipulation, and to some extent the benefits of hindsight history, the knowledge of eventual outcomes unavailable to the actors themselves. What is certainly clear is that on the day itself, whatever objectives and aspirations were invested in the storming of France's most notorious prison, few, if any, had the faintest idea exactly what was happening and what, consequentially, was about to unfold. It became a great day only in retrospect, albeit immediate retrospect: namely, as from 15 July, when the king went to the self-declared National Assembly to formally acknowledge its authority. From there the day proceeded to become a self-conscious Day, starting in the quick of revolutionary events themselves, with the first *Fête de la Fédération* on 14 July 1790, and culminating in the creation in 1880 of Bastille Day.

The hallowed place 14 July was to acquire in the annals of national memory was intended to be a place beyond controversy. Its theme was to be the unity of the People and the Republic, one and indivisible. But unlike 4 July, which, while subject to varying interpretations, has not been as such deeply controversial among Americans (few would see it as anything other than positive), the official versions of 14 July have masked profound disunities built into the remembering process itself, along with fierce disputes over not just its meaning but also its *value*. To take but two very well-known examples from the field of nineteenth-century historiography: for Michelet it was a glorious moment in the emancipation of the People, while for Taine it was but a spectacle of wanton destruction by the rabble (an 'excited and wild animal') and its subsequent remembrance a 'festival of murder'. Behind the public mask division has always been there, from the beginning through to the bicentennial, as faction and party, ideology and politics have scrambled to take 'ownership' of memory and adapt it to a present set of priorities.

There are many reasons why this is as it should be, not least that it exemplifies one of the things 14 July is supposed to stand for: a certain 'democratic' liveliness of debate, along with a rich array of registers – epic, tragic, ironic – for its depiction. Yet it has also proved to be something of an embarrassment for the official mythology. From this point of view, 14 July is supposed to stand, not for difference and division, but for national unanimity around the shared ideals of liberty, equality and fraternity. This has required the manufacture and projection of a consensus built in large part on the elision of what has made 14 July controversial: namely, the fact that it was a revolutionary *journée*. What on the historical ground was a massive disturbance of the peace must not be allowed to enter disruptively into the agreeably peaceful space of commemoration (not least for the reason that, if this were permitted, it might encourage further real disturbances of the peace). It thus becomes a matter of remembering the Revolution by forgetting what made it a revolution, burying the question Robespierre put with devastating clarity: 'Citizens, do you want a revolution without a revolution?' Whence the paradox of 14 July 1789 being consistently billed as a world-historical event while the very thing that made it, or its consequences, world-historical is equally consistently repressed.

To some extent, this is understandable. Presumably only a Robespierrist or the modern political equivalent could affectionately commend 14 July in terms of its being the day the 'people's decree' prevailed in the form of lynchings and decapitations. Certainly no sane person would want to follow through with Robespierre's logic to celebrating the Law of Suspects (forerunner of the show trial) and the reign of the guillotine. If there is any dignified form for representing this, it would have to be the idiom of tragedy, not epic (and perhaps only a Shakespeare could manage the Jacobin Terror). Nevertheless, Robespierre's characterisation of 14 July coincides very much with what 14 July was. One may or may not like this, but frankly neither affection nor hostility has much to do with it. It is not or should not be the task of the historian either to sentimentalise or to moralise history, and, whatever one's politics, it is a matter of plain historical record that violence was at the centre of the events of 14 July; it is what made the day a *journée*. If memory is to be not just another legitimation (or delegitimation) narrative, it has to be true to what is being remembered, however variously interpreted. Collective memory is not much good at this; it tends to turn its face away from what it would rather not see. In other words, collective memory is many things, including a contradiction in terms.

On the other hand, as a cultural force it has done its work with considerable success, the detail of which is the subject matter of the later chapters of this book. But alongside the operations of that commemorative machine, there has also been another force in play from the moment Bastille Day was declared a public holiday. This is the form in which, for the wider population, the festival has on the whole survived. In modern times the celebration of 14 July as a popular uprising has been largely confined, and even there but sporadically, to the politically militant districts of working-class Paris and other cities. Otherwise *le quatorze* today retains little felt connection with 14 July 1789. In its official guises it is pure display – a military defile, a presidential broadcast followed by a garden party in the grounds of the Elysée palace. Meanwhile, the general public to which the president's speech is notionally pitched, takes a break. The village streets of France are bedecked with tricolour flags and pennants, but it is extremely unlikely that the exploits of the *Vainqueurs de la Bastille* are uppermost in anyone's mind. At this level, the contemporary social reality of 14 July is close in spirit and practice to 4 July, both now simply a day of leisure for the majority of the working population. This has in no way damaged the remarkable elasticity of the political claims that can be made on either. President Bush, scrabbling around for bits and pieces to justify a democracy-exporting foreign policy, identified 4 July as 'the birth of democracy'. President Chirac, in his doomed attempt to persuade the French people to vote for the European Constitution, claimed the latter to be in direct descent from 1789. It is, however, doubtful that either ploy resonated deeply in the public imagination. In reality 4 July for Americans and 14 July for the French have become essentially a day off work, much prized if it happens to facilitate a long weekend. The politics of memory have migrated elsewhere: when Zhou Enlai said of the impact of the French Revolution that it was too early to tell what it has been, he was absolutely right, but he might well have been dumbfounded to see the truth of his observation verified in his own backyard. Who would have predicted the citing of 14 July 1789 by the protesting students on Tiananmen Square?

These domestic etiolations, the loss of original meanings even as origins are celebrated, are dispiriting but probably inevitable. Of the original day, Thomas Carlyle wrote that 'to describe this Siege of the Bastille (thought to be one of the most important in History) perhaps transcends the talent of mortals'. Happily, Carlyle did not inflict on himself the self-defeating position of taking literally his own words on the unavailability of words. The closest his fiery prose came to extinction was in the famous episode of the first draft of *The French Revolution* being consumed in the flames of John Stuart Mill's domestic hearth as the consequence of Mill's maidservant mistaking the manuscript for waste paper. Unfazed – he had no back-up copy – Carlyle sat down and wrote it again from memory. Carlyle was far closer to the events he wrote about, and, whatever one makes of his often hysterical politics, endowed with incomparable literary gifts.

As a story-teller, only Dickens, in *The Tale of Two Cities*, could hope to emulate him. Nevertheless, the place of 14 July 1789 in the historical record remains unique, and uniquely challenging to the powers of the historian (other than those who have had a vested interest in anaesthetising its significance). By contrast the Day, as something repeated from 1880 over a period of 125 years, no longer possesses anything like the same degree of glamour. Initially a spontaneously joyous as well as a politically engineered collective occasion, Bastille Day has, over time, come to look an altogether shoddier affair, progressively mummified into formal ritual orchestrated by assorted dignitaries, its culmination that extended piece of media kitsch, the bicentennial. Event and memory, ideally supposed to blend in a harmonious story, in fact have gone their separate ways.

That divorce is one of the principal themes of this book. On the other hand, it would be an error merely to lament the divorce, not just because of the unstoppably eroding effect of the work of time, but also because of the paradoxical relation between revolutionary event and the category of memory. In its purest ideological form, the Revolution wanted to sweep the past away and start anew from ground zero (Michelet thought that the only proper space of memorial for the Revolution was the Champ de Mars, not because it had been the site of festive occasion, but because it was, in his own time, an 'empty space'). Memorial was not logically the Revolution's natural ally, but the temptations proved too great and those involved fairly quickly sought to make it their friend. Shortly before his death, the radical Jacobin Saint-Just (basically Robespierre's right-hand man during the Terror) wrote a sort of testament in which he spoke of leaving a 'legacy to memory'. Where Saint-Just himself is concerned, memory has not, on the whole, chosen to respect his wishes (he has been comprehensively written out of the commemorative script). But, even discounting the particular case of Saint-Just, the wish itself, in its general form, sits oddly with the ideological and affective investments of the revolutionary actors themselves in the erasing power of the new.

And however one handles that intractable paradox, there remains the brute force of erosion, the ineluctable disenchantment that time brings to original enchantments. The nineteenth-century historian and thinker Edgar Quinet, commenting on Saint-Just's testament, observed, sadly but wisely, that modern human beings have limited resources for sustaining the 'contract' between event and memory:

> To give credit to the ideal Being, the Fatherland, to go so far as to accept the ideal recognition of future generations as payment for our services, who would want such a contract today?...This idea and all others of this kind have been extirpated from the human soul...They have become so alien and hostile that it is difficult to render them in a persuasive manner. Our present language refuses to express them. Yes, these ideas are dead.

There have been many attempts to rewrite the contract, many 'languages' of remembrance, some of them reputable attempts at fidelity to the original 'pledge' 14 July was held to embody, most of them, alas, travesties, reflecting for the most part the tawdry designs of politicians on increasingly inert national symbolic property. But before traversing the often debilitated landscapes of public memory, let us first go back to the extraordinary moment of the events themselves and what brought them about.

3. On 5 May 1789 the Estates-General convened at Versailles for the first time since 1614. The meeting came, with hindsight, to be seen as one of the founding moments of the French Revolution and of political modernity, a first step on the road to the creation of a sovereign National Assembly. In reality the occasion was fraught and inconclusive, the King making it abundantly clear that he had no intention of acceding to the more radical demands of the Third Estate.

3

THE CONVOCATION OF THE
ESTATES-GENERAL

The myth has it that 14 July 1789 embodied an absolutely new Beginning, but the events of that day did not of course occur *ex nihilo*; in historical reality, the mythical Beginning has its own beginnings, and, if we continue to see it as a uniquely pivotal moment, its intelligibility nevertheless rests on a plethora of antecedents, both regressive (through time) and expansive (across space). For example, the great historian of the taking of the Bastille, Jacques Godechot, has plausibly situated 14 July as a climactic moment in a history of uprisings that goes back to the social disturbances of the Wars of Religion and, in the context of the later eighteenth century, as having precedents and parallels on a large geographical canvas that includes America, Ireland, Belgium, Holland, London and Geneva. Things get even fuzzier when historical context is assimilated to the category of 'causes', which can all too easily spiral into the endlessly regressive. Yet causal analysis of what produced this extraordinary day is something that exercised even the eyewitnesses of the time, the very people one would have thought far too excited by what had been happening to command the requisite analytical detachment. In August 1789, Elysée Loustalot

– one of the most successful journalists of the early years of the Revolution – stated in the newspaper *Révolutions de Paris* that it was not enough 'just to give some arid account of certain facts'; it was also the duty of the contemporary commentator 'to go to the source of the facts and discover the causes of changes'. The following month he returned to this preoccupation, calling for 'a historical and political picture of everything that has happened in France since the first Assembly of Notables' as a basis for understanding 'the astonishing revolution that has just taken place'.

The Assembly of Notables was set up by the king's chief minister, Calonne, in February 1787 as a way out of an impasse in the negotiations between the royal administration and the *parlements* over tax reform. It failed miserably. What happened between then and 14 July 1789 supplies a causal crux with a twofold advantage. On the one hand, it breaks the otherwise unmanageable regress by bringing us as close as one can get to the events of 14 July while still retaining the distinctive character of causal antecedents. On the other hand, it shows how what began as the final spasm of a long-standing dispute between the crown and the nobility over the means of replenishing the depleted coffers of the state erupted into a fully fledged political crisis, involving not just who was to be taxed and by how much, but who had the *authority* to make these decisions.

The monarchical state, backed by the doctrines of absolutism, claimed that authority. The nobility, on the other hand, anxious to hold on to its privileges, claimed that there were limitations to royal power based on the laws and customary rights enshrined by the judicial institution that best served its own interests, the *parlements*. Had the conflict remained locked in this form, it is certain that, despite its institutional weaknesses at the time, the monarchy would have won – not because of the prestige of absolutism, but from the pressures of modern state-formation (a point magisterially developed by one of the greatest historians of the revolution, Alexis de Tocqueville). The frame of the dispute was, however, massively enlarged and complicated by the intervention of a third factor to which at the time the principal disputing parties had paid relatively little attention. This was what changed everything, with historical consequences that no one foresaw: namely, the increasingly vocal demands of the commoners (or so-called Third Estate). What began as a traditional relation between taxation and war (the right of the sovereign to levy the former to fund the latter) rapidly evolved into something quite different. The issue of taxation became indissolubly joined to the issue of representation and the question of sovereignty to the idea of a 'national' sovereignty, vested in neither the king nor the privileged orders, but in the People. This was also the formula of the American Revolution, but a more complex version of it: the issue was not just no taxation without representation (this is what the *parlements* had effectively been arguing in their resistance to the monarchy), but also the converse – no representation without taxation (emphatically what, in its more demanding forms, the *parlements* and the nobles did *not* want to hear).

The whole business started, then, as a problem of national debt, arising from the unsustainable costs of war (the Seven Years War, followed by France's involvement in the American War of Independence). These ventures were funded mainly by the taking out of loans, but repaying them in peacetime required further loans, thus generating the classic circle of creating new debt to service previous debt. Necker, the Swiss banker, who had been summoned in 1776 to act as director-general of finance, was a past master at manipulating the credit markets. In 1781 he published the first ever national accounts (the *Compte rendu au roi*), a wonderful smoke-and-mirrors job corresponding more or less to what today would be called 'off-balance-sheet financing'. But however adroit, this was no long-term solution to the burgeoning fiscal crisis. The law of no gain without pain could not be indefinitely suspended. Someone was going to have to pick up the tab for the consequences of military-imperial overstretch, and thus at some point the state was going to have to grapple with the thorny question of taxation. Necker resigned in 1781 and bequeathed the problems of squaring the circle to his hapless successors, D'Ormesson, Calonne and Brienne.

Their first move was on the sanctuary of Privilege. The wealthy aristocratic landowners were not only wealthy, they also enjoyed time-honoured exemptions from direct taxes as well as benefiting from equally time-honoured feudal dues from the labouring classes. Although in the course of the eighteenth century direct taxes were levied on many of the nobles, with the pattern of exemption thus becoming increasingly ragged, on the whole the system of imposition and evasion remained scandalously unjust. On the other hand, the fiscal crisis is not to be explained solely by the exemptions of the privileged orders; the chaotic state of the revenues was due as much to maladministration as to an unfair distribution of the tax burden. The economic power of many of the landowning aristocracy was ebbing, as exploitation of the land based on traditional methods became less and less profitable in contrast to the new methods of capitalist agricultural production (to which the more enterprising nobles, however, quickly adapted). Those who refused or failed to do so were in many ways a 'vegetating class', but this only made them altogether more anxious and defensive; the closer they got to ruin, the more they insisted on privilege and mobilised the *parlements* to protect them. In 1787 Calonne delivered an apocalyptic retrospect to the Assembly of Notables on how things stood: 'The coffers were empty, public securities devalued, circulation at a standstill; alarm was widespread and confidence had been destroyed.' This was of course but a prelude to billing himself as saviour. He saved nothing in all the relevant senses of the term, including the fiscal. The deficit he reported to the Assembly as out of control he succeeded only in worsening (he was popularly known as Monsieur Déficit).

Dismissed and exiled by Louis XVI in April 1787, Calonne was followed by Loménie de Brienne, who fared no better. In July the largest and most powerful of the *parlements*, the *parlement de Paris*, refused to 'register' (i.e. confirm) the financial edicts of the royal administration. Brienne at first stood firm, in August suspending and banishing the *parlement* to Troyes. He soon buckled. Six weeks later the *parlement* returned to Paris, amid scenes of jubilation and riot (the *parlements* mistakenly seen as defenders of the 'freedom' of all the king's subjects against the exercise of arbitrary power). Brienne withdrew his two main proposals for tax reform, replacing them with a scheme that was much lighter on the wealthy and much harder on the poor, to be accompanied by the raising of a new loan, which the *parlement* refused to register. By the spring of 1788, Brienne's ministry was blocked and the *parlement* had prevailed, and in the process had convinced large numbers of the common people that its version of 'liberty' was their liberty too (an illusion that had completely evaporated by early 1789).

Brienne's lack of political will was partly offset by the resolution of that much tougher political beast, the keeper of seals (roughly the minister of justice), Chrétien-François de Lamoignon. He was responsible for the framing and enforcement of the so-called May Edicts of 1788, the drift of which was to remove all legislative power from the *parlements* and to forestall resistance by stripping them of any powers whatsoever through the simple expedient of once more suspending them. As a more forceful repeat of Brienne's confrontation with the *parlements* the previous year, this was again interpreted as an assault on established freedoms. But by 1788 much had already changed. In some of the provincial *parlements* and assemblies both a new composition and a new political language were to be seen and heard. Lamoignon's suppressions sparked riots in Rennes, Besançon, Pau and Grenoble throughout the month of June, the most significant being the *journée des Tuiles* in Grenoble, which was followed by the gathering of the Dauphiné Assembly in the village of Vizille demanding a meeting of the Estates-General. What in 1787 had seemed merely fraudulent now began to resemble a genuine political alliance of *parlement* and people (even Robespierre, at the time still a lawyer in Arras, saw it in this way). In Paris there were violent protests against the Lamoignon edicts, along with the burning of effigies of Brienne and Lamoignon (the effigy, destroyed or paraded, was to become one of the leitmotifs of revolutionary demonstration). Yet if the mood had changed, the notion of an alliance of interests still rested on a misidentification. The freedoms championed by the nobles and the notables remained basically their freedoms and no one else's, least of all those of the common people. When the *parlements* were reinstated in September, they immediately reverted to form and showed their true face as bastions of privilege. By then, however, both Brienne and Lamoignon were thoroughly discredited, Lamoignon particularly hated as the king's strong man. In August Brienne and in September Lamoignon – though in his case well upholstered with a gratuity to enhance his pension so lavish as to exceed what actually remained in the exchequer – followed Calonne into the political graveyard (one year later Lamoignon disappeared for good into the real thing, having shot himself, although whether by accident or design is not known).

In many respects, all this was but the ministerial merry-go-round of appointments, resignations and dismissals presided over by a temporizing monarch, little more than an extended flurry of futile endeavour (Carlyle struck just the right note when he wrote of Brienne's fall from grace: 'Let us pity the hapless Loménie; and forgive him; and, as soon as possible, forget him'). An exception should, however, be made for Lamoignon, who is far more important to the story of the Revolution for the reason that he consistently, unambiguously and publicly identified the practical issue of the fiscal crisis with the principled question of political authority and legitimacy. When, in late 1787, the king called on the *parlement de Paris* to endorse further borrowing by the state, Lamoignon addressed the *parlement* in terms linking the issuance of a bond to the doctrine of divine right:

These principles, universally acknowledged by the entire kingdom, are that the King alone must possess the sovereign power in his kingdom; that He is answerable only to God in the exercise of his power; that the tie which binds the King to the Nation is by nature indissoluble; that the interests and reciprocal obligations between the

King and his subjects serve only to reassure that union;
that the Nation's interest is that the powers of its head
not be altered; that the King is the chief sovereign of the
Nation and everything he does is with her interests in
mind; and that finally the legislative power resides in the
person of the King independent of and unshared with all
other powers.

In November 1787 Lamoignon was speaking to the appropriate audience. There was, however, another waiting in the
wings whose arrival centre-stage he feared but whose historic significance he, like so many others, did not foresee.
Where the vacillations of Louis proved fatal to both the
ancien régime and eventually the monarchy, was in respect
of the one development that was to produce the greatest
irony in the causal skein that precipitated the outbreak of
the French Revolution: the convening of the Estates-General.
Brienne had reluctantly agreed to the convocation, at first
for some unspecified future date (he presumed it would all
fizzle out), then, on 8 August, for 1 May the following year.
The proposal did not come from the ministry, nor did it orig-
inate with the Vizille assembly. It was in fact the nobility's
idea, first floated by the Assembly of Notables in 1787. Faced
with deadlock in their running dispute with the absolutist
state over fiscal reform, they devised what they thought
was a smart ruse. Instead of continuing with the futile tactic
of refusing to 'register' royal edicts, the *parlements* were to
declare themselves 'incompetent' in matters of taxation. The
deadlock, they suggested, could be broken by the only body
that could properly decide the matter, the Estates-General,
which had not met since 1614. The Estates-General was an
institution that had evolved from its origins at the beginning

of the fourteenth century into a tripartite assembly in which representatives of each of the 'estates' – what very roughly we would call 'classes' – would convene at the pleasure of the king to discuss royal policy on matters of taxation. The belief of the Notables who argued for summoning it once more was that, if reconvened, it would proceed as in 1614, with the three orders (nobles, clergy and commoners) meeting in separate assemblies and voting as blocs; in this form, the two most powerful estates, the clergy and nobility, could combine electoral forces to frustrate the royal will. It was thus to be game, set and match to Privilege.

Its proponents, however, made one immensely conse-quential error of political calculation: they assumed the docility of the Third Estate. Little did they know that they were setting in train a sequence of events that would lead from the meeting of the Estates-General in May 1789 to the Third's self-declaration in June as a National Assembly and, after 14 July, both the king's recognition of the new assembly and the formal abolition of 'feudal' rights. Here was a classic case of history as unintended outcomes. For the Third Estate was no longer willing to be docile; if the Estates-General was to be summoned, its forms and terms of representation had to change. While the majority of nobles congratulated them-selves on their astuteness, the more far-sighted sounded warning notes. The duc d'Ormesson observed: 'You will get your Estates-General, and you will repent it.' More liberally inclined aristocrats, such as Lafayette, saw an opportunity. In his speech to the Assembly of Notables he described the proposal to convene the Estates-General as holding out the possibility for the 'convocation of a truly national assem-bly', alarming words to the likes of the reactionary comte d'Artois (the king's younger brother), who sensed that their clever ploy contained the potential for backfiring badly, his apprehensions a (for him rare) sign of political clairvoyance among a company of the blind. After Brienne's confirmation in August 1788 that the meeting would take place, Mirabeau declared: 'The nation has stepped forward a century in twenty-four hours.' But the decisive formulation of what this could and should mean was to be Sieyès' pamphlet of January 1789: *What is the Third Estate?* His own reply to the question of his title was to become the most celebrated formulation of its time: 'Everything. What has it been until now in the public order? Nothing. What does it want to be? Something.'

'Now that daylight is rising' (Sieyès' words), the movement from everything via nothing to something came out as a drastic recasting of the structure of political representation. It turned on three questions. First, what scale of representation was the Third to have in the Estates-General, given that the people it notionally represented formed the bulk of the population? Secondly, how was voting to take place – on the traditional model of separate assemblies for each of the three orders, each voting en bloc, or as a common assembly with representatives voting by head (i.e. as individuals)? Thirdly, how were the representatives within each order to be elected? The last question mattered in the sense that the multi-layered selection mechanisms governing the system of election within the Third ensured that its representatives were universally drawn from the professional classes, thus keeping workers and peasants at a distance. But this question was subordinate to the first two, which raised the grand issues of authority and legitimacy that were to yield the idea of a National Assembly in which power would be rearranged and redistributed.

The format for the articulation of these demands was the *cahiers de doléance* (grievance books). The input of the liberal professions was all about representation, the basis on which to meet and vote. At parish and district level, however (the level at which the peasant and labouring classes had access to the *cahiers*), the grievances were overwhelmingly about taxes and food prices, especially the price of flour, grains and bread (the staple diet of over three-quarters of the population). Peasant smallholders, agricultural workers and urban artisans had long been caught in an economic pincer movement between traditional privilege and capitalist modernisation, burdened on the one hand with 'feudal' obligations and, on the other, victims of new 'market' forces. The former included seigneurial dues paid to landowning aristocrats (the range was staggering, involving a whole nomenclature: *corvées, banalités, champarts, lods et ventes*) and tithes paid to the Church, deemed by both parties to be natural 'property' rights; the more fundamental 'natural' right – not to die of starvation – does not seem to have figured on the radar screen in quite the same way. During the 1770s Turgot, as controller-general of finances, had tried to rationalise the system by allowing prices to find their own level in a liberalised economy, while at the same time abolishing feudal impositions on incomes. The actual outcome was that the price of grain and bread rose, while incomes remained depressed by the continuing refusal of the nobles and clerics to forfeit their 'rights'. Turgot thus made enemies on all fronts. He dealt ruthlessly with the popular outbreaks of violence in 1775 known as the Flour Wars, while alienating the nobles by his efforts to dictate tax changes through royal decree. The king knew – one of the very few things Louis could be relied upon to understand – when he was on to a loser and dismissed

Turgot in 1776, though not without a prescient parting shot from the deposed finance minister: 'Do not forget, Sire, that it was feebleness that placed the head of Charles I on the block.' Necker was recalled, an experience to which he was to grow accustomed.

These social and economic inequities were compounded by natural as well as man-made causes, accidents of the weather and their effect on harvests. In 1770, 1772, 1774 and 1777 the harvest ranged from mediocre to bad. In 1788–9 it was close to catastrophic. The summer of 1788 witnessed the worst drought in living memory, with crops further destroyed by massive hailstorms; the countryside was commonly described as a barren desert. During the winter that followed, the trope shifted from Sahara to Siberia. The rivers and the mills froze. Travelling through Provence, usually blessed by the Mediterranean climate, Mirabeau recorded his impressions:

> one is tempted to say that the exterminating angel has struck the human race from one end of the realm to another. Every scourge has been unleashed. Everywhere I have found men dead of cold and hunger, bread often at five sous a pound, never less than three sous and seven deniers. In fact, people are starving to death with wheat all around them, for want of flower. All the mills are frozen.

In the spring of 1789 the thaw finally arrived, flooding the fields. In March grain and game riots erupted across the countryside.

The impact of this triple natural disaster – drought, freeze-up and flooding – was dramatic. Between the summer of

1777 and the early spring of 1789 the price of bread almost doubled. From the point of view of the poor, the question was no longer equity but sheer physical survival. One does not have to subscribe to economic determinism in historical explanation to see that the reality or dread of hunger (what the politician Barnave called 'the bread interest') was a key factor, and explains why food riots were to be a regular feature of the Revolution through to 1795, the issue of subsistence progressively infused with new forms of radical political consciousness; when in 1795 the *sans-culottes* invaded the National Convention they did so with the slogan 'Bread and the Constitution of 1793'. In the spring of 1789 the marriage of economics and politics was yet to be fully consummated, but the scale of the grain and game riots suggested that grievance had taken hold at a deep level. Meanwhile, in the towns and cities, artisans were threatened with falling wages and rising unemployment, partly as a consequence of a developing free trade in manufacturing equipment, most notably the new spinning machines imported from England (on 14 July, while the Bastille was being stormed in Paris, the spinners of Rouen were destroying the machines that had crossed the Channel; one of the minor ironies of history is that Danton's stepfather, a textile manufacturer, was a substantial importer).

This was the backdrop to the violent Réveillon riot that took place in Paris on 28 April. Réveillon was a 'modern' industrialist and also an Elector for the purpose of determining the city's slate of representatives to the Estates-General. His views were 'enlightened' in the Turgot mode, and at a meeting on 21 April to discuss his district's *cahier de doléance*, he had made a speech arguing that, with the removal of irrational and unproductive levies (most especially the hated customs tolls on goods coming into the city collected by the Farmers-General), both prices and wages would fall in tandem, thus generating the virtuous circle that was capitalism's formula for general prosperity.

Simplified and distorted reports of his speech were circulated, and widely interpreted as recommending a direct attack on wages. The workers at his factory in the faubourg Saint-Antoine reacted by destroying the factory. Although rumour vastly exaggerated the casualty figures, it was nevertheless a bloody affair that was to send shock waves through the city; fired on by troops sent to restore order, the dead and wounded were in the hundreds. Apart from the unprecedented scale of the violence, a further important feature of the incident was that it took place in the faubourg Saint-Antoine, an area of growing working-class militancy that was to be one of the hotbeds of 14 July. Although their concerns were primarily economic, the rioting workers were also heard to shout and chant political slogans; it was a sign that urban riot was about to mutate into insurrection. The first item on the morning agenda of the capital's *lieutenant de police* was to check the daily price of bread.

The second recall of Necker in the autumn of 1788 was supposed to be the magic recipe for defusing these tensions and conflicts. Although he could not be expected to control the weather, he was nevertheless generally perceived (largely on the back of his earlier repudiation of Turgot's draconian measures) as the People's Banker, the man who could be trusted to place controls on the price of grains and flour and dispose of the fiscal deficit by means of another virtuoso juggling of the nation's finances (he at least put his own money where his mouth was by lending the French state two million francs from his private fortune). It was also believed that he would further the cause of political reform. One of the first things he did on resuming office was to confirm that the Estates-General would meet the following May and that the representation of the Third Estate would be doubled. When, however, the deputies convened in Versailles, Necker's speech was something of an anticlimax. He uttered not a word on the other two demands of the Third Estate (common assembly and voting by head), less from cowardice, it seems, than from prudential considerations. Necker appears to have believed that a single assembly and individual voting would follow automatically from the concession of a doubling of the Third's deputies; why then provoke by making explicit what would happen naturally? This was to stake a reckless bet on the virtues of common sense. In any case, his speech was badly received ('a mind intoxicated with vanity, displaying an incapacity or unwillingness to explain or illustrate: a composition, indecent, unmanly, out of place, betraying a narrow understanding and a timorous heart', was one uncharitable judgement). As for the king's behaviour, he rejected the demands of the Third outright (speaking of 'a much exaggerated desire for innovations'), while going out of his way to make clear what he thought the proper place of the commoners was in the natural order of things.

Here was another confrontation between the king and his subjects, but this time involving a very different constituency, although one equally determined to have its way. From this point on, things start to unravel and to develop an unstoppable momentum. For a month or so not much happened in Versailles, basically a saga of inertia and delaying tactics.

Meanwhile, the price of bread in Paris continued to rocket (Necker's reimposition of price controls had not worked in the face of dwindling supply). Then on 17 and 20 June the Third Estate representatives make two declarations, whose performative force was to transform the French (and European) political landscape. On the 17th they announced their unilateral conversion into a National Assembly, with prerogative on all matters of taxation. On the 20th, locked out from their customary meeting place in the Salle des Menus Plaisirs, they repaired to the nearby royal Tennis Court, where, with one single abstention, they made the celebrated oath 'never to be separated until we have formed a solid and equitable Constitution as our constituents have asked us to do'. There was of course something incongruous to the greatest oath of them all, the gesture of political defiance that was to furnish the very ground of modern political legitimacy, occurring in a place of leisure and exercise (much favoured by the comte d'Artois, favourite of the queen and rabidly hostile to reform, who after the 20th made sure of booking the court for a week). But if symbolically incongruous, the mismatch of solemnity and locale was in no way historically odd, but rather an index of the improvised adaptations to contingency that is one of the hallmarks of revolutionary transformation.

Faced with the resoluteness of the Third, in late June the solidarity of the other two orders began to crumble. At first there was a trickle of defections. On 19 June, however, the clergy voted to join en masse. Yet the king and his advisers persisted in believing that the tide could indeed be rolled back. A *séance royale* for 23 June was decreed (to which the deputies of all three estates were invited), preceded by a private meeting with his counsellors at which the hard-line

views of the party of reaction were adopted. On the following day, the Third Estate was once more reminded of its pre-
ordained status (its representatives were herded into the hall
through a side door). The king spoke at (for him) considerable, even inordinate length. He then had read out a set of
statements and 'decisions', including the reminder: 'I owe
it to the commonweal of my kingdom, I owe it to myself, to
make you cease your fatal dissensions.' He then proceeded to
exacerbate dissension by flatly rejecting common assembly
('the King desires that the old institution of the three orders
in the state be preserved in every particular, as an essential
part of the constitution of his realm'). There may perhaps be
occasional collective meetings of the Estates-General, but, if
so, it was expressly forbidden to discuss both the form of
future meetings and the question of 'feudal and seigneurial
possessions, and the honorary prerogatives of the first two
orders'. In short, everything that had been raised in connection with the twin issues of taxation and representation was
to be kicked into touch, and to stay there for ever. The deputies were finally ordered to return to their separate assemblies: 'I command you, gentlemen, to disperse at once and
to go tomorrow, each to the chamber intended for your particular order.'

The deputies were stunned, the king leaving the hall
enveloped in silence (there was not a single utterance of
'Vive le roi'). The self-declared National Assembly refused to
disperse; flamboyantly defiant, Mirabeau threw down the
gauntlet: 'We are here by the power of the people, and we
will not leave except by the force of bayonets.' More ponder-
ously but no less firmly, Sieyès intoned: 'Gentlemen, we are
today what we were yesterday. Let us deliberate.' Protests
erupt, the crowd entering the courtyard of the royal palace,

where – in a first sign of shifting loyalties – the troops refuse to disperse them by force of arms. A text drafted by a number of *gardes françaises* soon enters circulation, *Avis aux grenadiers et soldats du tiers-état* (Announcement to the grenadiers and soldiers of the Third Estate), the predicate a bold act of sedition in its own right. Faced with such obduracy and determination, Louis backed off, dithered for several days and, on 27 June, recanted, 'instructing' the clergy and nobility to join the Third in common assembly (a bit late in the day, since the instruction was little more than ratification of what had more or less already occurred).

The developments from May through to late June describe an entirely new political constellation. The Third Estate now found itself caught in a two-pronged clash of wills, against both the nobles and the monarchy. The fear of an 'aristocratic plot' remained, but the frontline conflict was now with the king. What began as a contest between the monarchy and the two privileged orders became a struggle between the latter orders and the Third, and finally morphed into a dispute between the Third and the king. In other words, it was a chronology in which, broadly, the original form of the dispute was turned upside down, with the monarch facing a new antagonist. From the point of view of the monarchy, the juridical status of the meeting of the Estates-General was that of a 'consultation' between the king and his subjects, in which the king retained the authority granted to him by divine right. Initially the Third accepted this model, but by late June the stand-off was about an altogether new relation between representation and legitimate power. When in 1787 Lamoignon appeared before the *parlement de Paris* and made the speech in which he categorically stated that 'the King alone must possess the sovereign power in his kingdom', the *parlement* had its own reasons for not warming to this assertion. Had Lamoignon still been in office in early 1789, it is doubtful that the deputies of the Third Estate would have warmed to it either. Similarly, when also in 1787 the duc d'Orléans protested that the king's insistence that the *parlement de Paris* 'register' his fiscal proposals was 'illegal', Louis replied, first, 'I don't care' and, second, 'Yes, it's legal since it is my will.' The new audience for this doctrine was even less likely than the old to find this congenial. It was thus no surprise that the tergiversating monarch simply didn't know whether he was coming or going, nor that the new audience would turn a deaf ear, and finally express itself on the streets of the capital.

The picture of what causally and circumstantially led up to the events of 14 July is above all one in which a number of fault-lines across both the society and the polity became increasingly visible, with ever-growing pressure on all of them. First, there is a set of corporate interests prepared to use any means to resist the fiscal demands of the state. Secondly, there is the plight of the peasants and artisans, burdened by tithes and dues, at the mercy of weather-induced bad harvests, and the victims of the liberalisation of markets. Thirdly, there is a self-created National Assembly, determined but as yet of uncertain status and voice, without the backing of a constitution or formal recognition by the monarchy. Furthermore, having made 'representation' the key issue, it remained unclear what and whom exactly were to be represented. As largely a collection of middle-class professionals, along with dissident nobles and clergy, where would it stand vis-à-vis the grievances of the common people? The delayed and turbulent answers to that question would define most of the later course of Revolution in the great *sans-culotte* uprisings and the power struggle between Jacobins and Girondins. Finally, there was a royal administration bereft of coherent ideas, riven by faction and unsure where to place its bets. But it remained instinctively mistrustful of the newly vocal Third Estate, and when the chips were down very likely to side with Privilege. Taming the nobles in order to replenish the royal coffers and strengthen the authority of the state was one thing; siding with the rabble against the nobles was another altogether.

In the public imagination the reputation of Louis nevertheless continued to fluctuate in direct proportion to the fluctuations of his own position. On the one hand, he was the traditional protector, the argument for which had been put by the marquis d'Argenson, according to which monarchy and people were natural allies against the depredations of the barons. A recurrent refrain in the *cahiers de doléance* was the view of, and appeal to, the king as father of the nation. But this conception was now under considerable strain. For example, at the *séance royale* of 23 June Louis had prefaced his remarks by declaring himself 'the common father of all my subjects'. Yet a claim to fair-minded paternity looked increasingly threadbare as he proceeded to reject the demands of the Third, although there is evidence that he was in fact sympathetic to the calls for common assembly and voting by head and had simply capitulated before the pressures of the reactionary party at court. And where the common people were concerned, what mattered even more than politics was the price of bread; if, where the latter was concerned, the king's protection was not assured, then professions of 'love' for his people sounded increasingly hollow when, ducking and weaving as events unfolded, he seemed to have thrown in his lot with the party of Privilege. Stranded between the competing demands of those wanting to hold on to their privileges and those who wished to end them, Louis said one thing and then another; in a moment of private candour, he wrote: 'my greatest fault is a sluggishness of mind which makes all my mental efforts wearisome and painful'. Louis's other brother, the comte de Provence, put it more crisply: 'When you can hold together a number of oiled ivory balls, you may do something with the King.' Louis himself once observed – unhelpfully, one naturally presumes, but, given what he actually said, the presumption is questionable – that his silences mattered more than his words.

It is customary to stress the hesitations of Louis, as if his indecisiveness were causally decisive in determining eventual outcomes. But in fact they reflect more his sheer irrelevance, caught in an array of forces he was powerless to direct. Whatever he did, he was doomed to play a losing hand. Coping with the contradiction of appearing to want some sort of accommodation with the National Assembly and being unable to resile from what, in his understanding, made a king a king, irresoluteness was his only option. Up to a point, the people were prepared to give him the benefit of the doubt, in the form of conditional trust (the condition that was made explicit in 1791: 'Vive le roi, s'il est de bonne foi' – 'Long live the king, assuming his good faith'). But in early July 1789 that trust was stretched to breaking point. It was no longer merely a question of his prevarications but, more ominously, the fear of a double-cross. The outward concessions of 27 June perhaps concealed – as indeed they did – a secret plan for retraction and suppression. The decision to dispatch troops to encircle Paris was the truly bad sign. Why had the king authorised (if, probably, not himself initiated) a pre-emptive military move of this sort? Was it to contain the restive population of the capital? Did he have designs on the newly fledged National Assembly?

By now Paris was a tinderbox. There was no single spark and no single spot for what happened next, across a multiplicity of sites including the Palais Royal, the Hôtel de Ville, the faubourg Saint-Antoine, the Invalides and of course the Bastille. But it is generally agreed that the initial spark was the news of the sacking of Necker on 11 July (one contemporary observer described Necker's sacking as a 'thunderbolt'). Necker after all had been billed as a saviour. Even Robespierre had described him as 'a great man who seems to have been shown to the people merely for them to glimpse the full extent of the happiness they might enjoy, whose elevation was a triumph for genius, virtue and the nation'. What, then, did his dismissal portend – for the National Assembly in Versailles, the price of bread, the safety of Paris and its inhabitants? One of the choicer specimens of Louis's remarkable inability to think straight is to be found in the letter carried by his ministerial flunky La Luzerne, informing Necker that his services were no longer required: 'It is important to your integrity and reputation that there should be no cause for stir and commotion.' Stir and commotion were precisely what Louis's decision brought about, with huge consequences for the integrity and reputation of others than Necker himself.

These were the questions swirling in an atmosphere of uncertainty and confusion, along with the first intimations of a theme that would dominate the Revolution: fear of plots and treason. As news of Necker's ousting spread by word of mouth across the city on the morning of 12 July, Paris was abuzz with rumour. Rebellion was in the air, speeches were being made. And since the galvanising power of speech, both formal and informal, was one of the major causal instruments of the Revolution, capable of shaping all manner of outcomes (the three great leaders, Mirabeau, Danton and Robespierre, all understood that they were as nothing without speech-making), on the eve of the storming of the Bastille, let us repair in the first instance to that place of talk par excellence, the remarkable Palais Royal.

4. In this image the insurgents are more realistically attired, but the scene, as so often in Revolutionary iconography, is still a 'staged' one. The Bastille towers over the scene, a symbol of 'despotic' power, dwarfing but not diminishing the heroic purpose of the Common People, urged on by the man with the flag.

4

A LA BASTILLE!

Imagine a large piece of real estate in the centre of Paris, not only privately owned but – because privately owned – a place where the writ of the policing agencies did not run. There were many such agencies, so many indeed as to produce the complacent boast that in such a well-monitored capital incidents like the Gordon Riots of 1780 in London were inconceivable. However, the potential spanner in the works of this multiform apparatus was that unique late eighteenth-century urban site the Palais Royal. Originally Richelieu's estate, he bequeathed it to the crown, Louis XIV in turn ceding it as a private residence to his brother, Philippe, head of the Orléans branch of the Bourbons. When the latter's great-grandson, Louis-Philippe II, inherited it, he sought to demonstrate his 'democratic' credentials (during the Revolution he restyled himself Philippe Egalité) by opening the grounds to the general public. At the same time he redesigned the area as a zone of untroubled leisure and louche transaction, where virtually anything – most notably sex – could be bought and sold. By the time of the Restoration its logic had become entirely commercial (Balzac gives us an unforgettable description in *Illusions perdues*). But in the eighteenth century it also provided a home for the new-found attachment to untrammelled freedom of speech (it was the setting for the outrageously subversive dialogue that forms the bulk of Diderot's remarkable novel *Le Neveu de Rameau*). Here one could say what one wanted to say more or less with impunity, not least because Louis-Philippe, with political ambitions of his own, had an interest in appearing to side with radical causes. With its curious social mixes of strollers, gawkers, men-about-town, pedlars, prostitutes, *philosophes*, journalists, booksellers, rogues, plotters, spies and agents provocateurs, the Palais Royal was one of the most extraordinary gathering places of late eighteenth-century Paris.

When news of Necker's dismissal spread like wildfire on the morning of 12 July, it was naturally here that dissident and seditious opinion was at its most vocal. Danton had already been seen and heard there several times. Jean-Baptiste Poupart, who was to participate in negotiations with the prison governor during the storming of the Bastille, made a speech whose theme was that force must be met by force. But 12 July in the Palais Royal was above all the day of the young man who would die with Danton under the guillotine, the mercurial Camille Desmoulins, in whom a natural excitability turned easily to heady intoxication. Desmoulins, who had stammered since childhood, leapt on to a table in front of the café du Foy brandishing a sword in one hand and a pistol in the other, and proceeded, with passionate fluency, to speak of a planned 'Saint-Bartholomew of the patriots' (an allusion to the sixteenth-century massacre of the Protestants), and to demand that the people arm themselves against a corresponding threat by the king's troops. From the gardens of the Palais Royal the assembled crowd surged into the streets, growing apace as it made its way along the boulevard du Temple to the place Vendôme, where, at around 8 p.m., the first important skirmish took place (although there had already been sporadic outbursts of violence elsewhere in the city). A detachment of dragoons tried, but failed, to check the crowd, now numbering in excess of 5,000. The dragoons were rescued by the Royal-Allemand cavalry regiment under the command of the prince de Lambesc, who retreated to the place Louis XV while the crowd forced its way into the Tuileries gardens. Lambesc's men attacked but, under a hail of stones, were compelled to pull back.

The clash in the Tuileries gardens was in reality little more than a botched attempt at crowd control, with a handful of injuries and perhaps a single fatality. It became one of the triggering occasions of what turned into large-scale urban riot by virtue of what it gave rise to, that phenomenon which was to be an integral feature of the whole revolutionary landscape, with tremendous causal powers in its own right: rumour. Talk of a 'massacre' at the Tuileries travelled fast, no doubt exacerbated by the fact that Lambesc's cavalrymen were foreign mercenaries (French troops – the *gardes françaises* – rushed to the scene from their barracks to help the assaulted people). Here was confirmation of Desmoulins' predicted 'Saint-Bartholomew of the patriots', proof of a 'plot', or at least of a concerted plan to use military force to quell the population. Fear thus joined with grievance to convert a disturbance into an insurrection, animated by the slogan 'Arms and bread!' During the night of 12 July the principal action took place at the *barrières*, the tollgates at the city's walled periphery where customs duties were levied on all goods entering Paris (crucially grain and flour for the bakeries). While a reaction to the soaring price of bread, this too belonged in the conspiracy-narrative, echoing the ancestral popular belief in a 'famine plot' now suffused with a revolutionary anger reflected in the famous (and untranslatable) alliterative jingle: *'Le mur murant Paris rend Paris murmurant'* (haplessly, 'The wall enclosing Paris makes Paris murmur'). There had already been trouble at the *barrières* on 8 July (dealt with by Lambesc), but the violence on the night of the 12th was on a wholly different scale (forty out of fifty-four tollgates were demolished).

Meanwhile, in the city centre, throughout the night and into the next day, there was widespread looting – of the gunsmiths' shops for weapons, of the convent of Saint-Lazare for foodstuffs – along with the liberation of convicts from the Conciergerie and La Force prisons. From the point of view of the provisional municipality, 'anarchy' threatened, likely in turn to generate a crushing show of force from the royal troops encircling Paris. On the 13th the Paris Electors hastily constituted themselves as a permanent committee, presided over by the floundering and doomed Jacques de Flesselles, and moved immediately to form the *milice bourgeoise*, headed by the marquis de la Salle, that would shortly be named the National Guard. By the middle of the night 'authority' and insurrection combined to produce one of the most remarkable sights the capital had ever witnessed: a huge crowd assembled on the place de Grève (in front of the Hôtel de Ville) as in a torch-lit phantasmagoria, the defecting *gardes françaises* mingling with the common people and instructing the new civilian militia in the use of firearms. Besenval, meanwhile, had prudently withdrawn the royal troops to the Champ de Mars. But this did little to allay the power of rumour, which continued to circulate reports that the troops were already advancing into the heart of the old city, slaughtering 'patriots' as they went. However impressive the spectacle on the place de Grève, the weaponry in the hands of the insurgents was primitive, vastly more pikes than guns, and thus no match for the king's regiments. Guns, cannon and powder were imperatively required to stave off imminent disaster.

On the morning of the 14th around 8,000 Parisians, led by Ethis de Corny from the Hôtel de Ville, arrived on the esplanade of the Invalides, with a demand for arms known to be stored there. The governor, Sombreuil, denied their existence (having previously and futilely ordered his small band of infirm pensioner-soldiers to disable the muskets), whereupon Corny's official delegation was swept aside by a mass invasion of people who proceeded to ransack the stores, seizing twelve cannon and 28,000 guns, but few bullets and – critically – no powder. Corny's plan had been to take the requisitioned arms back to the Hôtel de Ville for orderly distribution to the militia. In the event, he retrieved only a fraction of the muskets, but all of the cannon pieces. Without powder, however, the latter were of no use. Some had already been secured: during the night a barge laden with barrels of gunpowder had been discovered at the port Saint Nicolas and taken to one of the bureaux of the Hôtel de Ville, where the indefatigable abbé Lefèvre spent the small hours distributing it, perilously by candlelight, the peril greatly intensified when – the tale is perhaps apocryphal – in wandered an inebriated member of the militia puffing on his pipe. When urged by the abbé to extinguish it, he drunkenly insisted on his citizen's right to smoke, the danger of everyone and everything going up in another kind of smoke defused only when Lefèvre offered to purchase the pipe.

But there was also the very large stock of gunpowder and ammunition that, on Besenval's orders, had been stored in the Bastille for safekeeping. As the events at the Invalides unfolded, a separate crowd from the faubourg Saint-Antoine and adjacent districts converged on the Bastille. This was as much about disarming the prison authorities as about arming themselves. As tension rose in the city, an anxious Launay had for some time been strengthening the Bastille's defences. In early July a detachment of Swiss mercenaries (from the Salis-Salamande regiment) had been added to the ineffectual standing force of eighty-two *invalides*. The embrasures holding the eight-pounder cannons had been widened, visible to all from the streets and – once again the effect of hearsay – interpreted as an indication of Launay's intention to attack the surrounding *faubourgs* at the earliest signs of trouble. Intentions were in fact mutually opaque to all parties, thus guaranteeing a high degree of contingency and unpredictability (the rest of the day was to be saturated with both). But out of this feverish brew of circumstance, supposition and panic began the process whereby 14 July 1789 was converted into the historic Fourteenth of July. Up went the cry, allegedly uttered for the first time by one Labarthe, a quartermaster to the *gardes françaises*, but in fact without determinate origin, echoing across the whole city, that was subsequently to resonate throughout the annals of the French Revolution: *A la Bastille!*

And so to the Bastille they went, in their thousands. What followed is the sequence of events that has been consistently named, and commemorated, as the 'storming' or the 'taking' of the Bastille (a practice which, out of deference to narrative custom, I myself have followed). Strictly speaking, this is a misnomer; the Bastille was not 'taken', it surrendered (it had done so on two previous occasions in the fifteenth and seventeenth centuries). Physically impregnable, its inner citadel could not possibly have been 'taken' by a crowd of demonstrators. Built on the orders of Charles V in the fourteenth century to guard the eastern approaches to the capital, it was originally a fortress rather than a prison (the term *bastille* was a common noun signifying 'fortress' or 'fort'). There were many *bastilles* across the land. The Parisian construction acquired both its upper-case designation as '*la Bastille*' and its fearsome reputation when, at the behest of Cardinal Richelieu, it became a state prison where persons could be sent and detained solely at the discretion of the king (on the basis of the infamous *lettres de cachet*). The overwhelming majority of *embastillés* were the victims of 'justice extraordinaire'. Because the latter practice bypassed all due process (the contents of the *lettre* were not disclosed and the identity of the prisoner was withheld), the Bastille was associated above all with secrecy: who, at any given moment, was there, and for what reasons, were unknown to anyone other than the monarch, his immediate advisers and the prison authorities (the *cause célèbre* being of course the Man in the Iron Mask).

Richelieu's successor, Mazarin, used it extensively to deal with the rebellious and seditious nobles of the so-called Fronde rebellion, while, after Louis XIV's revocation of the Edict of Nantes (which reinstated the civil rights of the Protestant community), it was also where large numbers of recalcitrant Huguenots were locked up. In addition to its political purposes as a place of detention for those perceived as a threat to royal power, it also housed perpetrators of economic crimes, especially forgers of the currency, as well as providing convenient incarceration for the black sheep of grand families, from the seriously delinquent to the insane (a private application by the family for the issuance of a *lettre de cachet* doing the trick). The aristocratic prisoners were, however, usually well treated, with ample provision of servants, good food, fine wines, furniture, pets, books and other amenities, such that for the privileged the Bastille often resembled more a hotel or a club than a jail (Marmontel congratulated it for the quality of its food, as if granting a star to a restaurant: excellent soup, succulent beef, marinated artichokes, vintage Burgundies and first-class Mocha coffee). The less privileged, on the other hand, were not so lucky, generally confined to the lower dungeons, where conditions were appalling.

During the reigns of Louis XV and Louis XVI, the Bastille continued to receive refractory and transgressing nobles, but there was a marked shift towards using it to punish and suppress the expression of enlightened opinion, especially the authors, publishers and distributors of prohibited and clandestine literature. Its more famous inmates included Voltaire, who had two spells in the Bastille, and the future leader of the Girondin party in the Assembly, Brissot, briefly imprisoned on his return from London for having published anti-government statements in his newspaper. Nevertheless, as a punitive instrument of state censorship, the Bastille, on the whole, exercised a light touch (Morellet even quipped that, for a writer, a sojourn on its premises was a helpful way station to acquiring both a reputation and a fortune), and in any case by the late 1780s it had become something of an expensive white elephant, with much talk of pulling it down.

Relative desuetude was, however, no impediment to incrustation by legend. Bastille literature had become something of a marketable genre, its circulation feeding directly into a collective view of the prison as a 'symbol' of unacceptable power. The two most widely read texts of the 1780s were the memoirs of Linguet and Latude. Linguet, imprisoned for the publication in London of his dissident *Annales politiques* and who appears to have experienced the prison in its more brutally squalid aspect, created a horrifying image of the Bastille as a 'devourer' of human flesh, but where the principal stress was on psychological rather than physical suffering, the prison as a place of existential annihilation and the deprivation of liberty as a radical dispossession of the sense of self; what was lost were not just a person's rights but the precondition of any rights at all, personhood itself. Latude, by contrast, con man and artist of the great escape, in his memoirs regaled the public with the saga of his multiple evasions. His story embodied the spirit of 'liberty' itself, a demonstration that the Bastille (and by implication the state machine it served) was not omnipotent. Along with Linguet's nightmare world of the self utterly at the mercy of secrecy and unaccountability, Latude's narrative contributed to the making of a political argument. The Bastille, it will be recalled, was not just a prison, it was a *prison d'Etat*. Already in the 1760s, the lawyer and jurist Antoine Servan had made the link between the practices of 'justice extraordinaire' and the doctrine of divine right, thus questioning nothing less than the foundations of the absolutist state (Louis XVI was distinctly unamused by the attack on the Bastille in Beaumarchais' *Le Mariage de Figaro*). Mirabeau, who had spent time in the Vincennes prison (where he met but disliked the Marquis de Sade), joined the argument in 1782 with his *Des lettres de cachet et des prisons d'Etat*. This was the background that enabled Michelet to claim that the siege of the Bastille was essentially a challenge by the Third Estate to arbitrary monarchical power.

This was, however, an exaggeration. On the day itself, the reality encountered by the besiegers when they finally penetrated the prison proved to be very different. The liberation of its prisoners was both accidental and incidental. More an afterthought than an express intention, indeed almost an oversight (initially, the prisoners themselves were completely forgotten when the keys to the cells were taken as a victorious trophy), the actual yield of freed inmates numbered no more than seven, although there was a nice symmetrical irony when, paraded in the Palais Royal later that night, they encountered their jailer for the last time, his severed head on a pike. The seven prisoners included one aristocratic delinquent (the comte de Solages, first imprisoned in 1765 at his father's request for 'infamous and atrocious crimes'), four forgers (La Corrège, Pujade, Bechade la Barthe and Laroche) and two lunatics: Whyte de Malleville from Dublin, first imprisoned at Vincennes in 1782 and transferred to the Bastille two years later, who oscillated between thinking he was God and Julius Caesar; and Tavernier, the illegitimate son of the financier Pâris Duverney, notionally a political prisoner (having been part of the plot to assassinate Louis XV), but who was spectacularly insane. There were in addition the 'fictional' prisoner the comte de Lorges (of whom more in a later chapter), and the infamous 'missing' prisoner the Marquis de Sade. Moved from Vincennes to the Bastille (his accommodation not just *tout confort* but *grand luxe*), the divine Marquis became nevertheless increasingly obstreperous. On his daily walk he took to rousing the passers-by from the faubourg Saint-Antoine with incendiary slogans; and, when his walk was suspended, he began to shout from his cell window that the governor had authorised the strangling of prisoners. An exasperated Launay finally had him removed to the asylum at Charenton in early July, writing to the minister Villedeuil: 'The whole staff would be obliged if you would accede to their wish to have the Marquis de Sade transferred elsewhere without delay.' On his release from Charenton, Sade restyled himself Citizen Sade, wrote several political pamphlets and became an ardent supporter of Marat.

⧗

As the crowd assembled in the course of the morning of 14 July, the image of the Bastille at the forefront of their minds was not that of a 'despot's' prison. Rather it had reverted to its former status as a fortress, its governor a military figure, appointed by the king and in league with Besenval to contain the population. Since it was widely believed that Launay was poised to attack the neighbouring faubourg Saint-Antoine with his cannon, the first demand was that the guns be withdrawn, and – in the name of self-defence – that the prison's store of ammunition and powder be handed over. These were also the principal requests of the first of a series of deputations from the Hôtel de Ville and elsewhere. A small group of lower-ranking officials arrived at around 10 a.m. They were cordially received by Launay and invited to join him for a meal. The governor agreed to the withdrawal of the cannon, but to nothing else (there is little evidence that he was pressed to do so). The repast must have been convivial, since it lasted an hour and a half, during which the crowd grew substantially larger and, when swollen by the large numbers from the Invalides, altogether more restive. At this juncture the demands escalated: what was now required was the surrender not just of the contents of the Bastille but also of the Bastille itself. The latter was mutating fast into a 'symbol' and the issue becoming one of 'authority'. The increasingly tense atmosphere was also exacerbated by fears that the munching and quaffing delegation had been taken hostage. Some of the demonstrators set off for the nearby district of Saint-Louis de la Culture to report these fears.

The consequence was a second deputation and a major change of tone. It was headed by Thuriot de la Rosière, future deputy in the Convention (the more radical successor to the Legislative Assembly), member of the Committee of Public Safety and, as Robespierre's arch enemy, instrumental in the latter's downfall. Thuriot's meeting with Launay was nothing like as convivial. Imperiously high-handed and irascible, with a thunderingly loud voice, Thuriot did not attempt so much to negotiate with Launay as to intimidate him. He also upped the ante even further by requiring (not requesting) Launay to place the Bastille in the hands of the civilian militia. Since for Launay that amounted to treason, he naturally refused (Launay was many – largely unpleasant – things, but his loyalty as a servant of the crown was unimpeachable). He did, however, confirm that the cannon had been withdrawn and invited Thuriot to make a tour of inspection. Thuriot appears to have believed Launay's declaration of peaceful intent, but his own domineering attitude succeeded only in worsening the situation, with various unintended outcomes. As he left the Bastille, he disdainfully neglected to inform the crowd of the upshot of his dealings with the governor, a silence that was misread as betokening a sellout; this was a first indication that the breach between 'authority' and the 'people' was to implicate the people's representatives as well as the king.

Thuriot made his way to the Hôtel de Ville to give an

account of his dealings with Launay, from where he was sent back to the Bastille to calm the crowd with the announcement that Launay had agreed not to attack if not himself attacked. He was about to set off when sounds of explosion and gunfire were heard. A dead body is carried in; cries of 'vengeance' come from the place de Grève. Thuriot had bungled his first mission, and his second was destined to fail utterly; when he finally got back to the Bastille, he encountered a scene of such chaos that it proved impossible for him to get inside, let alone take charge. The crowd by now had become a throng, gathered in the outer precincts of the prison (the Cour du Passage) but pressing forward to gain access to the first of two courtyards, the Cour du Gouvernement, which was the site of the governor's lodgings. Access was secured by a moat and two drawbridges, one for pedestrians and the other for carriages. Both drawbridges were raised.

What happened next was one of the two cruxes of the day's events. A couple of young day labourers, Davanne and Denain, climbed on to a shop roof on the north side of the Cour du Passage, and from there, followed by Pannetier, a grocer, Tournay, a carter, and Bonnemère, a soldier, they crossed the ramparts down into the Cour du Gouvernment in search of the guardhouse keys. Unable to find them, they grabbed axes and smashed the pulleys of one of the draw-bridges, which, as it crashed down, killed one and wounded several. The crowd poured into the courtyard, shots were fired (who opened fire first was to be endlessly disputed, the eyewitness testimony marked by irresolvable claim and counter-claim); within a few minutes there were nearly 100 dead sprawled out on the ground, mowed down by the defending Swiss Guards.

It was now around 2 p.m. In the space of four hours

the situation had changed dramatically. As things spiralled out of control, there was a third deputation headed by Delavigne, the president of the Assembly of Electors. Delavigne and his colleagues (most notably the enterprising abbé Fauchet) came with a triple demand: a ceasefire; the surrender of arms and munitions; and – a compromise version of the earlier proposal from the intransigent Thuriot – admission of the militia to work alongside Launay's band of veterans and Swiss Guards in protecting the garrison. Here was a formula for defusing the conflict and imposing some sort of order, in the form of a deal between two sources of 'legality'. The formula did not get even to first base; in the noise and confusion, the delegates were neither heard nor seen. It was all very different from the studiously polite, quasi-ceremonial reception of the first delegation earlier that morning. The firing continued, with further casualties and, from the enraged crowd, a new call – for the 'destruction' of the Bastille itself and 'death' to its governor. In practice this meant entering the inner courtyard, also secured by a raised drawbridge. But this was a task of a different order of magnitude. The inner courtyard was the true citadel of the prison. Launay did not have many troops (and, lacking in foresight, very few provisions), but he had almost unlimited ammunition and of course the cannon on the towers. With the resources at the crowd's disposal, this was an unassailable position. Some carts packed with straw had been brought from Santerre's brewery in the faubourg Saint-Antoine and set alight to provide a smokescreen as cover from hostile fire in the attempt to press forward into the inner courtyard. But even if they had succeeded in lowering the drawbridge, what awaited them would have been nothing short of a massacre (although they did not know it, a cannon had been moved into position just behind the entrance gate from the drawbridge).

Had the situation remained like this, the whole business of 'storming' the Bastille would probably have ended in a stalemate, and the dispersal of an exhausted and ragged throng. It certainly would never have become what it is famed for (a successful siege) without a further crucial development. The abortive third delegation returned to the Hôtel de Ville, where more dead and wounded were being brought in and the able-bodied were calling for arms. The Electors decided to try yet again with a further delegation consisting of Ethis de Corny (now back from the Invalides), Poupart, Boucheron and Piquod (Boucheron was to provide an eyewitness account of this episode), this time accoutred with official regalia, a flag and a drummer. Boucheron and Piquod managed to get into the Cour du Gouvernement, where they persuaded the crowd to stop firing, advanced to the drawbridge and shouted up to the troops stationed in the towers that they had come to negotiate, but on condition that there be not just a ceasefire but a laying down of arms. For a moment this seemed to be working, the veterans in particular giving every sign that they wanted the situation to end. And then suddenly the attempted negotiation collapsed (according to the insurgents, because Launay refused to cooperate). The first round of cannon was discharged from one of the towers, accompanied by a volley of musket fire. There were more fatal casualties. The delegates, blamed by the crowd for this turn of events, beat a hasty retreat. It was at this juncture that the pivotal transformation occurred, with the intervention of troops from the *gardes françaises*. Up until now the efforts of the municipality to impose its will on both the crowd and the governor (its progressive escalation of demands making it by extension a contest of power with crown) had been a tissue of failures. With the arrival of the troops, a riot which had turned violent became something more like an organised military assault; it was also the moment when the symbiotic relationship between the Revolution and the Soldier was born.

The *gardes françaises* were an elite corps, but this meant that their senior officers were even more distant from the common soldiers they commanded than was the case in the foreign regiments. Moreover, since they were garrisoned in Paris, everyday contact with the population affected their sympathies and loyalties; one of their tasks was to police the theatres, in the course of which they picked up many a proto-republican maxim from the plays being performed. Defection was in the air. After the *séance royale* of 23 June, when the crowd had gathered in front of the palace at Versailles to demonstrate in support of representatives of the Third Estate, the *gardes françaises* refused to use force to disperse the demonstration. Two days later around 3,000 *gardes* swore an oath in the Palais Royal to protect the National Assembly and fellow 'citizens'. On 30 June a group of soldiers was arrested for insubordination and taken to the Abbaye Saint-Germain prison, where they were freed by invading demonstrators, the troop detachments sent to stop them not lifting a finger (Thomas Jefferson, then the United States minister to France, wrote that the troops had been arrested 'on account of their dispositions in favour of the national cause'). During the clash in the Tuileries on 12 July, several troops went to the aid of the people under attack by Lambesc's detachment of German mercenaries, later followed by an exchange of fire between loyalists and deserters in which lives were lost on both sides. The night of 13 July was a time of widespread defections, and when the Hôtel de Ville constituted itself as a permanent committee, the allegiance of deserting *gardes françaises* (many of whom were already active in the districts) was greeted with joy.

Among those imprisoned at the Abbaye were Pierre-Augustin Hulin and Jacques-Job Elie. Both were to play a major part in the rest of the day's events. Hulin, a former non-commissioned officer and currently director of the Queen's Laundry, showed up around 3 p.m. on the place de Grève (he had already been one of the speakers at the Palais Royal on 12 July and on the morning of the 14th was at the Invalides, rallying defectors), where he found two detachments of *gardes françaises*, to whom he delivered a passionate, tear-stained harangue: Launay and his men are murdering 'our fathers, our parents, our wives and children ... I swear I will bring you back victorious or you will bring me back dead'. Accompanied by thirty-five *gardes*, 300 armed militia and four cannon, he made his way to the Bastille, where he was joined by Elie, a second lieutenant in the Queen's Infantry, who had also come from the place de Grève with a contingent of *gardes françaises* originally assembled by Sergeant-Major Wargnier, Sergeant Labarthe and Sergeant Richemont, who invited Elie to take command.

Hulin took charge of firing cannon at the Bastille walls (not very effectively, the walls being too thick). More audaciously, Elie attempted to bring down the drawbridge leading to the inner courtyard. He ordered the removal of the carts of burning straw, which, while useful as a smokescreen, also assisted the garrison forces in blocking access to the second bridge (two of Elie's comrades were killed in the attempt). Two cannon were brought into the Cour du Gouvernement and trained on the raised drawbridge. Faced with these developments,

Launay panicked. He wanted a signed capitulation and a written guarantee of safe passage for him and his guards. Without that assurance, he threatened to blow up the whole place with the gunpowder stocks. He tried twice to get to the storeroom, but was prevented by some of the *invalides* (most notably Bequart, who was shortly to be grimly rewarded for his efforts). Having restrained Launay, and knowing the game was up, they cried out 'Surrender,' and flew a white handkerchief. The besiegers appear not to have picked up any of this, although they were aware that the gunfire had ceased. They advanced to the bridge. It was not yet 5 p.m.

And then suddenly it was basically over. Through an aperture in the drawbridge gate negotiations were opened, with a Swiss Guard proposing 'honourable' surrender. This was rejected. The guard then passed through a piece of paper with Launay's terms (guaranteed safety or he blows the Bastille to smithereens). Planks were thrown across the moat, an unknown assailant tried to retrieve the piece of paper and fell into the moat. At the second attempt, Stanislas Maillard managed to get hold of it and handed it to Elie (not Hulin, as sometimes reported). Elie accepted the truce terms on his 'word as an officer', but the crowd wanted none of it. At that precise moment, however, the bridge was lowered and the gate opened by the *invalides* (they later claimed that had they known what was to happen next, they would not have done so without a written agreement signed by officials from the Hôtel de Ville). First on to the bridge was Grenadier Arné, followed by the others, who surged into the inner courtyard, where most of the garrison troops were stationed, the Swiss Guard on one side, the veterans on the other. But there was still some firing from the towers. The enraged crowd erupted into a frenzy of vandalism.

The principal object of their fury, however, was the 'traitor' Launay. One of the assailants, Claude Cholat, claimed to have been the one to capture the governor, but it was in fact Maillard who, aided by Arné, handed Launay to Elie and Hulin. The latter felt bound by the code of soldier's honour and due process, but the crowd wanted Launay killed on the spot. The *gardes françaises* managed to get him out of the Bastille, although he was already wounded and bleeding profusely. Elie and Maillard left to head a victory cortège to the place de Grève and the Hôtel de Ville, while Hulin remained with the crowd jostling around Launay. Exhausted, Hulin decided to pause for rest and a restorative glass of wine. It was a fatal error. When he rejoined the crowd, he found Launay's head already on a pike. The governor, it seems, did not take kindly to role reversal and was not a cooperative or docile prisoner. Abusing his captors ('chienne de populace' – 'bitch of a people' – apparently the expression he used) was in the circumstances imprudent, although a declaration of undying love for the People would have got him nowhere either (Foulon tried this tack to no avail). As they arrived at the place de Grève, Launay put up a struggle and kicked one Dénot (or Desnot) in his 'republican parts'. This was the cue for instant and gruesome butchery. Bayoneted in the stomach, savagely stabbed over and over again, he was finished off with a bullet to his head. There remained the business of parting the head from the body. The honour fell to Dénot, a cook fired for drunkenness and theft and very much a last-minute revolutionary. Dénot tried to cut off the head with a sword, but, having botched the job, he took a kitchen knife from his pocket and hacked through what remained of Launay's neck. He later described his endeavours as a patriotic act for which he should be given a medal.

Shortly thereafter, on the place de Grève itself, Launay's adjutant, Losme, was slaughtered, while several other Bastille officers were strangled in the rue des Tournelles. Soon it was to be the turn of Flesselles. As *prévôt des marchands*, his basic loyalties were to the *ancien régime*, and it was only under pressure and with great reluctance that he had accepted the formation of a provisional municipal government with Third Estate representation. The crowd that returned to the place de Grève triumphantly bearing Elie was in ugly mood. A message came through from an insurrectional committee based in the Palais Royal that Flesselles, accused – although the record is unclear, it seems with some justification – of having concealed arms that had been promised to the militia, was to be escorted there for an improvised 'trial'. As he came out on to the steps of the Hôtel de Ville, he was shot, his head cut off and stuck on a pike to join that of Launay.

Just over a week later it was the turn of counsellor of state Foulon and his son-in-law, Berthier de Sauvigny. If Launay's death was frightful, it was nothing compared to what was meted out to Foulon. Appointed as controller-general of finances after the dismissal of Necker, he was widely hated, mainly because he was alleged to have said that the food rioters 'were worth no more than his horses; and that if [they] had no bread [they] had only to eat grass'. Having fled the city, he was captured, made to walk barefoot back to Paris, a bundle of hay tied to his back, given vinegar to drink and his sweat wiped off with nettles. Once back at the place de Grève, and despite Lafayette's entreaties, he was dragged across the square and strung up on a lamppost. The rope snapped twice, so they finished him off by severing his head and – now standard practice – impaling it on the end of a pike, with some of the hay stuffed in his mouth. His heart was also ripped out (by none other than Dénot). Heart and head finally ended up in a tavern at the Palais Royal, where they were thrown out of the window. Berthier, meanwhile, was lynched after having been forced to kiss the severed head of Foulon.

Robespierre, it will be recalled, dignified the rough justice of Foulon's murder with the name of the 'people's decree' (Barnave was even more glacial when he asked rhetorically: 'Was their blood so pure?'). But there were also the cases of no justice of any kind. Only the mix of confusion, panic and paranoia could explain the awful fate that befell the heroic Bequart, the veteran who had prevented Launay from blowing up the Bastille and, like Humbert on the other side, the victim of a double misidentification. On opening the gate to the inner courtyard, his hand was cut off at the wrist still holding a key and, in the belief that he was one of the prison warders, displayed on the streets as a trophy. A few hours later, mistaken for someone who had fired the cannon at the crowd in the Cour du Gouvernement, he was dragged by the hair to the place de Grève, where he was hanged.

These are the grim footnotes to the day's events. As night falls, the city is gripped by the terrified anticipation of reprisals from Besenval's troops. All Paris is out on the streets, everywhere barricades are being erected and patrols are circulating; everything and anything to hand is being used to improvise arms – pikes, stones, hot ashes (with which to blind enemy troops), boiling oil and water. The Bastille is a continuing scene of looting and vandalism. In essentials, however, the day's drama has played itself out. Indeed the analogy of a 'drama' in several acts is one for which the historian often reaches as a retrospective shaping device. The rush of events can be given a perfectly intelligible design when seen as punctuated by the four deputations and structured by the two critical turning points: the lowering of the first drawbridge and the invasion of the outer courtyard; then the arrival of the *gardes françaises* and Launay's capitulation. But this convenient ordering edits out the sheer scale of fast-flowing mishap, chance and randomness of the type we encountered in Humbert's report; as another eyewitness put it with masterly understatement: 'It cannot be denied that there was much confusion and disorder.'

First, there were the many misunderstandings and communicative mis-hits, the most consequence-laden being what took place when the chains of the first drawbridge were smashed. Unable to see Davanne, Denain and the others, the crowd mistakenly believed that the drawbridge had been lowered by Launay's men, an error further compounded when, as they poured into the courtyard, the *invalides'* yelling from towers an order to retreat was interpreted as 'enter' – a literally fatal misunderstanding for the many who lost their lives. Then there were the several insurgents who, having swarmed into the towers and appeared in the embrasures, were taken for garrison troops and fired on by their own people. When Launay surrendered, Hulin was taken for the governor and nearly sliced in two by a sabre. Clouet, the senior administrator in charge of the stocks of gunpowder and saltpetre, was also mistaken for Launay and was only saved from certain death by Vielh, at great risk to his own life. Misidentification extended to one Mlle Monsigny, the daughter of the veterans' commanding officer, who, believed to be Launay's daughter, was saved by Bonnemère in the nick of time from being run through by a pike and then burned alive (for this exploit Lafayette personally conferred on him a sword of honour). Misreading and misrecognition could also spin from near tragedy to pure farce: the Swiss Guard were twice taken for Bastille prisoners, once inside the Bastille itself and then later when, to thunderous applause, they were displayed in the Palais Royal.

These were but the accidents of perception and interpretation of a cognitively dishevelled scene. Cognitive mayhem was, however, further intensified by the pervading atmosphere of suspicion and mistrust, and not just where one would naturally expect to find it, between the opposing camps. Launay's alleged 'treachery' made him of course the villain of the piece (when he removed the cannon the crowd thought they were being reloaded), and the carnage in the outer courtyard was held, erroneously, to be the outcome of a dastardly deception, proof that Launay was the agent of a wider 'aristocratic plot'. For his part, Launay was quite capable of reciprocating. The officer of the Swiss Guard, Deflue (who wrote one of the more reliable eyewitness accounts), described Launay as both incompetent and paranoiac ('He was so terrified at night that he mistook the shadows of trees and other objects around him for enemies'); he was especially convinced that the Corny delegation was the setting of a 'trap'. But the most notable instances of potentially life-threatening misconstruction occurred within the camp of those notionally fighting for the same cause, above all in the relations between the besiegers and officials from the Hôtel de Ville. Flesselle's apparent mendacity made him, in the eyes of the besiegers, a sort of mirror-image of Launay, and it is thus no surprise that they shared the same fate. But even those who sought to act in good faith fell under a cloud of suspicion: Thuriot's *hauteur* was misread as betrayal, while the efforts of Corny's deputation to persuade the crowd to pull back were interpreted as connivance with the prison authorities. We have also seen how Humbert almost lost his life when mistaken for one of the enemy.

Happenstance, paranoia and random violence are thus central elements of the story of 14 July 1789 that the epic myth has tended to elide. Conservative historians, on the other hand, have emphasised them as the essential elements, the stuff of which *the* story is made. For every Jean-Baptiste Humbert there was no doubt a Dénot (another drunkard, Soudain, added to the idiom of the macabre in making off to the morgue with the heads of Foulon and Berthier in order to wash them before they were stuck on pikes). Yet out of the chaos and madness of the day something genuinely revolutionary was achieved. The following day the king accepted Liancourt's advice to go forthwith to the National Assembly to announce the withdrawal of his troops. The announcement was tantamount to a formal recognition of the powers of the new assembly. Two days later he came to Paris, where he was greeted by the new mayor, Bailly, and handed a tricolour cockade. Bailly welcomed him with the following words: 'Sire, I bring Your Majesty the keys of your good city of Paris. They are the very ones that were presented to Henri IV; he had reconquered his people, and here the people have reconquered their king'. This was not intended as a provocation, but it is difficult to imagine that the king could have heard Bailly's words as anything other than an explicit reminder that the grounds of sovereignty had shifted and that the days of absolutism were gone for ever. Mirabeau spoke of the collapse of an 'antique edifice'; it was not merely a building – the Bastille prison – that he had in mind.

By day's end the besiegers were already collectively entering legend as conquering heroes. Four days later, Maillot, a deputy at what by now had been renamed the Constituent Assembly, wrote to Desbroux that they were a group of men virtually without 'shoes and stockings' who in the space of forty-five minutes had seized the most powerful place in the kingdom. But who exactly were they? Some became household names overnight. Hulin and Elie were given entries in the *Petit Dictionnaire des Grands Hommes*, published in 1790. Joseph Arné, the carpenter who had enrolled in the *gardes françaises* and had been instrumental in handing over the captured Launay, acquired instant fame. On 15 July he was driven through Paris in a triumphal chariot. Along with Humbert, he figured in dozens of popular ballads and broadsheets. He was also the principal character of the first play on the storming of the Bastille, staged in September 1789, *La fête du grenadier*. Arné was himself present at the première, and at the end of the performance, in a nice convergence of fiction and reality, he appeared on stage with the actor to standing ovations. The English press, as ever intent on discrediting the Revolution, put it about that he had entered the Bastille only to save a mistress.

Some went on to important roles in the later chapters of the Revolution. Léonard Bourdon became president of the Jacobin Club and, along with Thuriot, was instrumental in engineering the downfall of Robespierre (he was the leader of the armed group sent to arrest Robespierre). Fréron, the ardent regicide and revolutionary activist, after having enforced the Terror in the provinces with particular brutality, also joined the anti-Robespierre camp. Maillard presided over the 'sort of tribunal' set up at the time of the September Massacres. Santerre made a buccaneeringly roguish career in the National

Guard, turned a blind eye to the September Massacres, was central to the 10 August coup and was the militia officer who escorted Louis XVI to the guillotine. Parein Dumesnil became a committed republican and was implicated in the Babeuf conspiracy (though he was acquitted). Joseph Souberbielle, the surgeon, found himself on the jury at the trial of Marie Antoinette. Rossignol became one of Danton's right-hand men. The abbé Fauchet was arrested in 1793 (on 14 July!) as a Girondin, confessed his 'crimes' and was subsequently executed. Poupart de Beaubourg became an agent of the Girondins and of Lafayette, describing Jacobinism as a 'pestilential miasma', and is alleged to have invented a form of invisible ink for the purpose of secret communication.

Yet 14 July 1789 was not the day for those who were about to become or already were major players. Some of the latter showed up later, as tourists. The young deputy Robespierre arrived with other members of the National Assembly on a sightseeing expedition (it is said that he caught the future Madame Tussaud as she slipped on the stones), and conveyed his thoughts in a private letter: 'I could not tear myself away from the place; the sight of it produced such feelings of pleasure and ideas of liberty in all good citizens.' The man of the hour, Mirabeau, arrived in a carriage bedecked with flowers strewn by a mass of supporters lining the streets. Once inside, he demanded the grand tour, especially keen to visit the dungeons. He departed laden with the gift of books and papers mouldering in the cellars. One likes to think they may have included copies of Mably's *Des droits et des devoirs du citoyen*, issued in late 1788 after nearly thirty years gathering dust. Lamoignon, the keeper of the seals, fearful of its 'incendiary' reputation, ordered it seized and had 1,600 copies buried in the dungeons of the Bastille.

As for the individual whose hour had not yet come, during the night of the 16th a certain Captain d'Anton (as he then styled himself) of the Cordeliers district militia turned up with a particular objective in mind. Around 11 p.m. on the 14th, the marquis de la Salle had nominated the elector Prosper Soulès as temporary commander of the Bastille, in a vain attempt to keep some kind of order. Danton had other ideas about keeping order and dragged Soulès off to the Hôtel de Ville to have his papers verified. Lafayette had to intervene to clear the matter up (in Soulès' favour; Soulès provided a written account of this disagreeable experience, but was to undergo the even more disagreeable experience of perishing under the guillotine in 1794). Here was an early example in a minor key of Danton's understanding that the only way to occupy a power vacuum was by the exercise of brute force (the policy which underlay his most famous utterance: 'Dare. Always dare. And again, dare. In this way you will save France').

These, however, were but walk-on parts, after the event. The overwhelming majority of the besiegers both emerged from and disappeared back into near-total obscurity. Our only source of information about most of them is their appearance in the official catalogue of the *Vainqueurs de la Bastille*. The baptism was not without controversy and much tasteless wrangling. It took the form of a list of names, or rather several lists, the variations reflecting the competitive and sometimes unscrupulous efforts to get on it. The title of *vainqueur* was a coveted term of official recognition from the point of view of winners' history, a term with which to strike a claim to ownership of a great event. Initially there was some reluctance to be entered, less from modesty than from fear of reprisal on the part of those not yet sure they were on the winning side. But restraint did not last long, especially when it became clear that not just fame and glory but also material recompense were in the offing. Cousin Jacques (the pseudonym of the journalist Beffroy de Reigny) started a list but gave up in disgust when confronted with a number of claimants hugely in excess of the actual participants (in his *Testament* he denounced them as liars and intriguers).

There were three other lists. Maillard, who became secretary of the Vainqueur organisation, compiled his own and included 662 names. Dusaulx, the Paris elector, headed a committee of four (the others were de la Grey, Oudart and Bourdon de la Crosnière) charged with devising an official register. Its deliberations were conducted in open session. This created a space for deal-making, in which individuals and groups mutually conspired to attest the presence of one another. To help in processing the depositions, the committee enlisted the help of Bonnemère, Cholat, Elie, Goisset, Hulin, Maillard, d'Osmond, Rousselet, Thuriot and Tournay. The list quickly ran to 871 names, with many false claimants. Exasperated by the scale of dishonesty, the Hôtel de Ville referred the matter to the Constituent Assembly, which raised the tally to 954 (in part by virtue of inadvertently listing various candidates twice).

Yet despite all the wrangling, fraudulence and mutual recriminations, the lists remain a useful, if limited, source of information. This is especially true of Maillard's, which identified 634 persons by trade and address as well as by name, thus enabling at least a rudimentary sociological description of the besieging crowd. Based on these sources, an early twentieth-century study (compromised, however, by its thesis that the storming of the Bastille was basically a Freemasons' plot) discloses a mixture of social classes.

There were some students, writers, radical clerics, a handful of middle-class rentiers and assorted foreigners. But by far the largest number consisted of working people: tradesmen, small workshop masters, journeymen artisans, day labourers and unemployed from the working-class *faubourgs* close to the Bastille. Many, especially carpenters and cabinetmakers, were of course from the faubourg Saint-Antoine. Yet its importance has been exaggerated, contributing to the forging of yet another legend – the so-called 'myth of the faubourg Saint-Antoine'. A leaflet of 21 July, *Les lauriers du faubourg Saint-Antoine*, stated that 'it is undisputed that the fatherland owes its salvation to the citizens of the faubourg Saint-Antoine' (Carlyle was to use the term as shorthand for an Ur-version of the *sans-culottes*).

Most of the participants, however, hailed from the neighbouring, and poorer, districts: Petit-Saint-Antoine, Saint-Louis de la Culture, Saint-Paul and Les Enfants-Trouvés. Leaving the professional soldiers on one side (who were initially classified separately as *Volontaires de la Bastille*), they were cobblers, jewellers, gauze-workers, dyers, masons, nailsmiths, hatters, tailors, locksmiths, hairdressers and wigmakers, printers, braziers, upholsterers, potters and stovemakers. They include Etienne Georget, one of the first to use the cannon, and who was shot in the thigh; Toussaint Groslaire, wounded in arm and leg and who, while lying on the ground writhing in agony, is alleged to have declared to his wife that his injuries were 'nothing, my dear, what is my life worth compared to the salvation of 24 million?'; Louis Guignon, the tailor who brought the Bastille register to the Hôtel de Ville on the tip of a bayonet; Mercier, the wine merchant from Saint-Paul, who helped Elie remove the lighted wagons and sustained several wounds in crossing the plank to receive from the Swiss officer the terms of Launay's capit-ulation; Laurent Pelletier (or Peletier), about whom all that is recorded is that he was stricken with a hernia during the siege; Antoine-Charles Perrin, the journeyman carpenter, also wounded and whom Reigny described as 'a small man, of feeble health, but whose patriotism produced strength and vigour'; and Louis Tournay, the eighty-two-year-old who jumped from the adjoining roof into the Cour du Gou-vernement and released the chains of the drawbridge. There was one woman, the laundress Marie Charpentier, who fought like a lion and was one of the twenty-five to get a pension for having been rendered lame from her wounds. Another source speaks of 'une fort jolie femme' trying to restrain her lover from joining the fray, but when he refused she quickly changed into men's clothes and fought alongside him. And how might the bliss in that dawn to be alive have seemed to what appears to have been the youngest of the participants, an eight-year-old boy, Lavallée, the petit Gav-roche of the storming, who, according to the account he gave later to Guffroy, was one of the first to scale the towers?

Compared with the abundantly documented lives of the Revolution's big hitters, these are but crumbs from the his-toriographical table, scraps gleaned from a largely empty or depleted archive. Indeed in respect of most of the *Vainqueurs*, what we have is next to nothing. The following entry in the list is typical: Baron, *gazier* – a surname, a trade (gas worker) and then a blank. This is of course both tantalising and frus-trating for the historian in search of the past, but there is also something affecting about the archival silence inhabited by these shadow profiles. There is, moreover, a paradox here: in one crucial respect, we learn more from what we don't know about the historical significance of the *Vainqueurs* than from what we do know. For while it is true that our relative ignorance is a reflection of limited records, it is also the case that the principal story to tell is not of individuals but of a genuinely collective action. It is the first major appearance on the historical stage of the Third Estate as the People.

The latter proved to be a fluid, often dangerously labile term, and was from the outset a subject of controversy. When Mirabeau argued that the elected members of the National Assembly should be designated 'representatives of the French people', it was objected by the lawyers that the word could be taken to mean either the *populus* (the people as a whole) or the *plebs* (the lower orders). This was not just hair-splitting jurists' talk. Not only at the level of ideology and discourse, but at that of deed and action, the Revolution was to a very large extent the (increasingly fraught) negotiation of these two meanings, one ecumenical and 'fraternal', the other more laden with connotations of class antagonism. In the heady atmosphere of 1789 it was by and large the first meaning that prevailed. Even Marat, before casting himself as the spokesman of the plebs, joined the ecumenical party when, in his *Offrande à la patrie* (written in February 1789), the Friend of the People described the People in the inclusive idiom of cross-class allegiances:

The French third estate is composed of the class of servants, mechanics, labourers, craftsmen, shopkeepers, commercial agents, merchants, farmers, untitled landowners and stockholders, schoolmasters, artists, surgeons, physicians, men of letters, scholars, lawyers, magistrates of the lower courts, ministers of the altar, army and navy – a numberless, invincible legion containing within its breast both wisdom and talent, strength and virtue.

To some extent the actors of 14 July embodied this cross-section, but the bit of Marat's description that captures the essential social reality is its first part. This is why we know so little about them; they belong to that form of history 'from below' sometimes called *historia abscondita* (the history that is lost to us as forever veiled). In his account of the storming of the Bastille, Michelet consistently uses the impersonal pronoun *'on'*. In this context it does not adequately translate as the English 'one', but is rather the grammatical sign of anonymous collective agency, with a strong connotation of heroically sustained purpose, a trope designed to move and exhort rather than an accurate historical observation designed to inform (the counter-trope was Burke's 'swinish multitude' and the reference in *The Scarlet Pimpernel* to 'the surging, seething, murmuring crowd...human only in name'). But in an important sense Michelet got it right: even when stripped of its intended meaning (the People as Hero), and restored to its evocation of the indeterminate, the pronoun does the requisite work: the true dramatis persona of that historic day remains the *on*, which, however idealised and mythologised, lies in the record as stubbornly mute.

PART TWO: MEMORY

5

THE *FÊTE DE LA FÉDÉRATION*

In a pamphlet of 1788, Camille Desmoulins, sensing what lay just round the corner, exhorted his small band of readers (the pamphlet was circulated in handwritten form): 'Patriotism spreads day by day, with the devouring rapidity of a great conflagration. The young take fire; old men cease, for the first time, to regret the past. Now they blush for it.' After 14 July the blushing time was over. In the minds of most, the *ancien régime* was strictly *ancien*, finished. The past that mattered was not last year but yesterday, and it was indissolubly linked to what might and should lie ahead: the Revolution triumphant. Hot on the heels of the literal 'yesterday', Antoine-Louis Gorsas, the editor of *Courrier de Versailles à Paris*, wrote: 'Yesterday will be forever remembered in the records of our history: it opens the way to the greatest and perhaps the most fortunate revolution.' In similar spirit, the ubiquitous contemporary commentator Louis-Sébastien Mercier composed a 'Farewell to the Year 1789', whose peroration brought memory, or more accurately the prospects for memory, centre-stage (Mercier's text has been neatly described as an exercise in 'preemptive nostalgia'): 'Great year! You will be the regenerating year, and you will be known by that name. History will extol your great deeds.'

This was relatively quick off the mark, so fast indeed as

5. With the overthrow of the monarchy on 10 August 1792 and the
declaration of a republic shortly thereafter, the former date came to replace
14 July as the official commemorative date. The new festival was sited on the
re-baptised Place de la Révolution (before the Place Louis V, now the Place
de la Concorde). Demachy's painting shows the ritual burning of emblems of
royalty.

to evoke a paradox in being concerned more with the future of memory than with its object in the past. Proleptic talk of this sort about how 14 July would be remembered was common in the immediate aftermath of the Bastille episode, and it points to one of the more intriguing difficulties faced by the historian of the French Revolution in distinguishing between 'events' and their commemoration. The latter process started immediately, inside events themselves, and may be said to have contributed in some measure to the subsequent development of the Revolution as it moved into new stages. Strung out across memory and desire, prospect and retrospect, the already accomplished and things yet to be accomplished, the capture of the Bastille came to occupy an unusual temporal grammar in which past, present and future tenses jostled alongside one another. Much later, in the twentieth century, Charles Péguy collapsed the temporal distinctions entirely, arguing that the storming of the Bastille was its own instant commemoration, its 'zero anniversary' ('the fall of the Bastille, history tells us, was strictly speaking a festival, it was the first celebration, the first commemoration and, so to speak, the first anniversary of the fall of the Bastille. Or, in a word, its zero anniversary').

The dominant medium for this instant commemorative flurry was, of course, that of print, above all the sudden explosion of journalistic ventures, as reportage simultaneously straining for the monumental. In one of the best known of these, *Révolutions de Paris*, Loustalot reached as early as 17 July (it was the newspaper's first issue) for the language of memorialising hyperbole: 'this glorious day…the triumph of justice and liberty'. And so it went on, in similar rhetorical vein, across the whole terrain of a feverishly improvised print world. Hyperbole is close to the making of fictions, and the one strayed into the other at the hands of the remarkable Jean-Louis Carra. Carra was one of those ferociously energetic oddballs that the Revolution regularly threw up, as if at random. In pre-revolutionary times, he was, like Marat, a scientist of sorts (particularly interested in the physics of electricity). Also like Marat, at the outbreak of the Revolution he became a journalist and with Mercier founded in October 1789 the *Annales patriotiques et littéraires*, probably the most successful and widely read of all the revolutionary journals (it was especially popular in the provincial Jacobin Clubs). Himself a fervent Jacobin, Carra was subsequently elected as a deputy to the Convention, although these radical affiliations did not seem to inhibit his wilder ideas, such as the proposal that the French monarchy be handed over for safekeeping to the Duke of York.

In his guise as journalist, the inventive Carra immediately cottoned on to the marketability, both financial and political, of Bastille tales, and, in association with his inaptly named *Mémoires historiques et authentiques sur la Bastille*, he published a short book called *Le Comte de Lorges* (the non-existent but legendary prisoner said to have been liberated from the Bastille on the 14th). The 'authentic' was at a premium in this business (Latude was to title his own memoirs *Mémoires authentiques*), but few could rival Carra for sheer chutzpah: as a measure of the veracity of his story, Carra claimed to have met with and questioned the Count on his release (and prior to the all too convenient disappearance after which he was never to be 'seen' again); nothing could be more 'eyewitness' than that, and thus at a stroke a purely fictitious personage was spirited into the realm of attested historical memory. Brought to life as a figure of testimonial, the Count was given an exhortatory speech in which memory, wish and prophecy converged on the theme of festival: 'I want to celebrate for ever, yes, I desire that the Fourteenth of July be a day of festivity in eternity.'

The comte de Lorges also found a place in a medium that was in some ways even more important than print, if only for the reason that it was accessible to the illiterate. The future Madame Tussaud, Marie Grosholz, officially the niece but probably the daughter of the Swiss impresario Philippe Curtius, who ran a waxworks establishment in the boulevard du Temple in Paris, made a model of de Lorges. Curtius effectively invented the recipe that was to be the staple of waxworks exhibitions (the combination of the famous and the villainous). His most renowned show was mounted – where else? – in the Palais Royal in the 1770s, featuring such Enlightenment luminaries as Voltaire, Rousseau, Necker and Benjamin Franklin. He was also employed to make wax funeral effigies in the classical style. For Voltaire's cortège organised by Jacques-Louis David, he produced a model to accompany the corpse swathed in vermilion robes. Naturally, it rained, and the vermilion dye stained the effigy, thus inadvertently plastering an early form of modern kitsch on the attempted revival of an ancient funerary tradition.

The effigy was to have a more macabre role in the economy of both action and representation before and during the Revolution, variously paraded, mock-executed or burned. Indeed to this day on the far left it retains something of its revolutionary force; on the night of Nicolas Sarkozy's election as president, protesters who had gathered at – of course – the place de la Bastille burned an effigy of the successful candidate. Straw replicas of Brienne and Lamoignon were consumed by fire in front of the statue of Henri IV on the Pont-Neuf, as were the straw-doll copies of Réveillon and

Hanriot during the April riots. Wax, however, was a more durable (and a more potent) medium, and for a time Curtius's shows became a mix of running commentary on events (what much later in the nineteenth century, in connection with the Paris waxworks, was to be called a 'plastic newspaper') and a form of propaganda, a means of inciting the populace to patriotic thoughts and deeds. This was to take a grimly recursive turn, circling from wax to human, back to wax. On 12 July 1789, inflamed by Desmoulins' speech in the Palais Royal, the crowd demanded from Curtius the wax busts of their heroes, Necker and the duc d'Orléans, to carry around the streets as a gesture in support of reform. Two days later it was the turn of the victims, the decapitated Launay and Flesselles. Within hours of their removal from the pikes, the heads were rushed to Marie; in her memoirs she records taking the impressions while seated with the bloody heads on her knees. Naturally, when the guillotine went into overdrive, there were heads galore, supplied by both the enemies of the revolution and the Enemies of the Revolution. The most popular collection featured wax busts of Louis XVI, Marie Antoinette, Carrier, Fouquier-Tinville, Robespierre and Hébert, with, in the foreground, Marat in his bathtub (later Madame Tussaud claimed that David used her work as a model for his *Marat assassiné*).

But all these efforts pale into insignificance when compared with the entrepreneurial tenacity of that one-man memorial machine, Citizen Palloy. After the capture of the Bastille, Palloy, a master builder by trade who had done very well out of the Paris construction boom of the previous two decades, was immediately commissioned to supervise the demolition of the hated prison. This was not quite the symbolic act of bidding farewell to the *ancien régime* it seemingly resembled. Demolition had been on the cards for some years, the expense of its upkeep held to outweigh the prison's usefulness. Several argued that it was better to retain it as a reminder of despotism, while the actual reason for ordering its destruction was the practical, if unfounded, fear that, by means of a series of hidden tunnels, it might be reoccupied by the king's troops. On 15 July Palloy arrived on site with a large contingent of building labourers to dismantle the edifice, stone by stone (the task was more or less completed by the following November).

Palloy was, however, an ardent patriot as well as an enterprising building contractor (he was officially listed as one of the *Vainqueurs* on the basis of a somewhat dubious claim) and conceived the idea of using the materials of the prison for commemorative purposes. The idea was to develop over the years into a veritable culture industry, mixing sentimentality and fetishism on a grand scale: inscribed slabs and plaques made from the Bastille stones, memorial medals, miniature models of the prison, paperweights, dominoes (made from the marble that had adorned the governor's windowsills), replicas of Latude's rope ladder, a stone bearing a chiselled portrait of Mirabeau and another inscribed with the Declaration of the Rights of Man and the Citizen. The project was of course partly designed as a money-spinner, but Palloy's primary motive was less mercenary than political (his obsession was to ruin him financially), dedicated to disseminating memorabilia across the whole of France as a way of binding together the national-patriotic community: 'It did not suffice for me to have participated in the destruction of the walls of this fortress, I had the desire to immortalise the memory of its terrors.'

⧖

Most of Palloy's efforts had as their backdrop the revolutionary festival, both unofficial (often initiated by himself) and
official, starting with the first *Fête de la Fédération* on 14 July
1790. As early as 18 July 1789 Voltaire's protégé Charles Villette (originally a marquis, he burned his letters of nobility)
had called for a publicly institutionalised celebration of the
fall of the Bastille. Spontaneous festivity had already broken
out in the course of 1789, especially in the provincial towns
and cities. The most noteworthy event in Paris was a procession in mid-September from the faubourg Saint-Antoine to
the church of Sainte-Geneviève, led by a contingent of the
National Guard carrying a miniature Bastille made from
cardboard, along with papier-mâché images of the wounded
and the dead. Towards the end of the year, the thought that
there might and should be a national festival on an annual
basis, to take place on 14 July itself, began to gather pace.
In December 1789, Clément Gochon, a worker from the faubourg Saint-Antoine, submitted a proposal to the Commune,
Projet d'une fête nationale pour être exécuté le 14 juillet 1790,
and, with Palloy at his side, suggested that its centrepiece
be a huge balloon, each of its four sides to be painted with a
representation of the great events, from the invasion of the
Invalides through the storming of the Bastille to the king's
journey to Paris on 17 July. Bailly approved, stating: 'We
suggest that this meeting [...] be sworn on the next 14 July,
which we shall all see as the time of liberty: this day shall be
spent swearing to uphold and defend it.'

The institution of a national festival was, however, properly the remit of the Constituent Assembly, not least because
it was anxious to retain control of popular demonstrations,

no matter how joyous. The last thing it wanted was a repeat of the revolutionary *journée* itself, although Mercier was to write that the truly great festivals were the *journées* themselves, 'barbaric festivals' bathed, as in ancient Rome, with the stench of carnage. The Assembly began the process of sedulously eliminating all allusion to raw violence. In June 1790 it approved the demand forwarded from the Commune (with Talleyrand as intermediary) for a 'general Federation' to take place on 14 July. It was to be called a festival of federation in order to include all the municipalities of France and the regionally federated branches of the militia (as head of the militia, Lafayette, with an eye to the starring role, insisted on a strong military colouring to the proposed event).

The further decision to hold the festival on the Champ de Mars (at the time outside the city limits) created a problem that was in turn to become something of an occasion, in its own way the actual heart of the construction, both literal and metaphorical, of communal memory. The plans were not finalised by the Constituent Assembly until 21 June. With just over three weeks in which to make preparations, the Champ de Mars was subjected to a renovation blitz. The field, already a quagmire from the heavy June rains, had to be levelled, terraces to seat 400,000 had to be built, along with a triumphal arch, an Altar to the Fatherland, and a grand pavilion in which to seat the king and his party. Despite employing 15,000 workers, it became clear that the work could not be completed on time. And so was organised that gently fraternal version of the *journée*, the so-called *Journée des Brouettes* (the Day of the Wheelbarrows). We do not know who made the suggestion, but, as of one mind, the people of Paris, from duchesses to dustmen, priests and soldiers, rich and poor, along with thousands of delegates from the provinces, repaired to the Champ de Mars to dig, shovel and shift. It was backbreaking work; indeed the field had to be not only levelled but also lowered by several feet in order to ensure the visual prominence of the Altar to the Fatherland at its centre. But the work, it seems, was conducted in a spirit of genuine cooperation and good humour. In terms of egalitarian goodwill, the high point of the festival was attained before the festival itself properly speaking began. 'It was there,' wrote Mercier, 'that I saw one hundred and fifty thousand citizens of all classes, ages and sexes making the most superb picture of concord, labour, movement and joy that has ever been witnessed.' This of course was Mercier in characteristic overdrive, but his picture was not a mere travesty of the facts.

The first *Fête de la Fédération* was conceived as a 're-enactment', not of the actual events of 14 July 1789, but of their 'meaning', understood as the founding moment at which the social 'contract' that sealed the Nation as a unified entity was drawn up and proclaimed. Hegel famously remarked that history repeats itself, the first time as tragedy, the second time as farce. If that is so, it is a law that applies *a fortiori* when the second time round is history as re-enactment. The Russian anarchist Kropotkin (who wrote a history of the French Revolution) described it as 'one of the most beautiful popular festivals ever recorded in history'. But to a large extent he must have consulted the records with his eyes half shut. Impressive it might have been as a choreographed event, but the one thing the authorities could not predetermine was the weather. It poured, in buckets, nearly all day long. Around 8 a.m. the assembled National Guard, along with the provincial delegates, the Commune deputies and regulars from the army and the navy, proceeded from

the boulevard du Temple (presumably past Curtius's waxworks and of course past the site of the Bastille) to the place
Louis XV, where they were met by the representatives of the
Constituent Assembly as well as an assortment of foreign
dignitaries ('Swedes, Spaniards, Polacks, Turks, Chaldeans,
Greeks,' as one source has it); there was also, authorised by
the Assembly, a delegation from the United States which
included Tom Paine. Crowds lined the streets in their thousands, singing the revolutionary 'Ça Ira', in some sort of
counterpoint to military drumbeat and salvo. Militia, Army,
Assembly, People were as if fused in a collective celebratory
affirmation; Paris had never seen anything like this before.

They were also soaked to the skin. Numbering well in
excess of 100,000, the bedraggled but still enthusiastic procession reached the Champ de Mars, by now a sea of mud,
several hours later, entering the field through the strategi-
cally placed Arc de Triomphe, to a correspondingly triumphal shout of welcome from the waiting spectators (an
estimated 260,000 Parisians). It took another hour or so
for the procession to file in, and around the middle of the
afternoon formal business began in unrelentingly atrocious
conditions. The ceremonial focal point was the Altar to the
Fatherland, suitably adorned with patriotic image and text.
First came the 'Mass' (which has to go into inverted commas,
not least because it was officiated by that parody of a churchman, the Bishop of Autun, who specialised in never showing
his face in Autun, Charles Maurice de Talleyrand-Périgord).
Talleyrand didn't believe a word of what he uttered; one
story has him begging Lafayette at the altar not to make him
laugh, and after it was all over he repaired to more agreeable precincts, the private gaming table of a high-society
vicountess, where he proceeded to take all the players to the

cleaners. Apart from the difficulty of keeping a straight face, there were also the impediments of rain and wind, his robes sodden, incense that wouldn't burn, his voice more or less inaudible, but at least they had the merit of stripping away some of the layers of charlatanism.

Yet somehow he got away with it, delivering in pseudo-religious garb the essential revolutionary-federative message of the New Dawn ('on this day France has been made anew'). Indeed it is a remarkable feature of both this and other revolutionary festivals that they drew extensively, if eclectically, on bits and pieces of religious paraphernalia. Palloy, for instance, called his Bastille stones 'patriotic relics' and his miniature Bastilles 'votive sculptures'. Even more bizarrely, according to one contemporary newspaper account, the National Guard in one of the Parisian districts presented the local church with 'consecrated bread of considerable size in the shape of the fortress of the Bastille'. Mercier was later to fulminate: 'No idols, no idolatry in our Republic'. But revolutionary iconoclasm, along with the more general aversion to external signs of 'difference', had a hard time extirpating deeply rooted attachments to religious symbolism. Robespierre expressly resisted much of the later 'de-Christianising' phase of the Revolution and was personally responsible for that strange revolutionary invention, the Festival of the Supreme Being.

The Mass was, however, but a prelude to the Oath, with this time Lafayette as the star performer. Where Talleyrand just about managed it, Lafayette provided fabulous theatre. Battling the elements, he rode his trademark white charger from the altar to the pavilion where the king and his family were placed, humbly asking His Majesty's permission to swear the oath of 'federation'. Having both obtained permission and appropriated majesty, he rode back to the altar, itself adorned with various images and slogans, the most important bit of text trinitarian in character: 'The Nation, the Law, the King'. Having taken the precaution of distributing a very large number of surrogates around the field to declaim in unison with him (the inaudibility problem), he drew his sword, advanced to the altar and declared:

> We swear to be forever faithful to the Nation, to the Law and to the King, to uphold with all our might the Constitution as decided by the National Assembly and accepted by the King, and to protect according to the laws the safety of people and properties, transit of grains and food within the kingdom, the public contributions under whatever forms they might exist, and to stay united with all the French through the indissoluble bonds of fraternity.

The oath was then successively repeated by members of the National Assembly and the gathered multitude. As for the king, Louis had arrived late, and remained in his pavilion, conspicuously aloof from the whole proceedings. He did, however, swear his own oath, to use 'all his powers' to defend and uphold the (as yet unwritten) constitution. Sceptics parsed this as ambiguous, in the sense of Louis intentionally implying that his powers in this regard might prove strictly limited. On the other hand, whatever he meant by the oath, he was obliged to declare it as 'King of the French' (not 'King of France'). The change spoke volumes, signifying an end to the mystical bond of monarchy and territory underpinned by the doctrine of divine right; it was not long before he would be simply referred to as Louis Capet. Marie

Antoinette then rose to her feet, holding the young dauphin aloft and declaring (presumably between gritted teeth): 'This is my son, who, like myself, echoes the same sentiments.'

Despite the weather-induced debacle, the festival was carefully planned and monitored. Of all the proposals submitted to the organisers, only three were approved: the procession of the militia, the mass and the oath, all three related components of a consciously orchestrated ceremony. The most resonant was the oath, its general importance as a secular-political ritual captured by the art of David in the unfinished sketch of the Tennis Court Oath, but above all in that earlier and prescient masterpiece of oath-taking, the *Horatii*, with its tensed arms converging on a single point in pictorial space. The *Fête de la Fédération* reproduced that pattern on a mass scale, the right arms of all present raised and directed towards the centre occupied by the altar, the physical expression of a common allegiance. In principle the oath engaged the whole 'nation'; in reality, as well as ceremonially, it was the affair of the *fédérés* of the National Guard, an early form of the new cult of the citizen-soldier and the militarised *patrie*. When not playing at churchman, Talleyrand got it right when he observed: 'It is France armed that is going to gather together, not France as a deliberating body.' Notionally, the festival was about the militia *and* the people, bonded as on the day of the storming of the Bastille. From the point of view of those controlling the festival, however, it was to be primarily about the militia *rather than* the people. Behind the façade of a theoretically all-inclusive consensus, the structure and meaning of the *fête* were to be defined and organised by a hierarchical system of subordinations and exclusions.

The officially excluded category was of course the

Aristocrat, minus the large number of enlightened nobles, such as Lafayette, who had cast their lot with the Third Estate. Symbolically, the Aristocrat fulfilled the role of the ritual scapegoat. But the exclusionary logic also extended to the People (as the potential troublemaker). The People figured as an abstraction, but not the people as such. They were present as spectators rather than as participants, kept at the edge and on their best behaviour within a rigorously calibrated pecking order. Keeping the People out or at the margins was one of the concerns implicit in the extensive 'topographical discussions' on how to arrange bodies relative to the Altar of the Fatherland. The official visual symbol (along with the federative flag) was a triangular design representing Nation, Law and King. But in the placings of the audience around this symbol of egalitarian concord, some were clearly more equal than others. The disposition of persons was shaped as a set of concentric circles: the inner circle for the soldiers and the militia, the next for assorted political notables and the outer circle for the assembled multitude. This was the true image of France reborn.

After the 1790 festival, Mirabeau rationalised these arrangements and their meanings in a programmatic treatise on the subject, in which he made it quite clear that civic obligation was to come before popular exuberance, and that since carnival was associated with riot, appropriate methods of containment and control were to be the order of the day. This was intended to detach festival from festivity. The popular *fête*, when it took place at all, occurred elsewhere, especially in the provinces, and, when left to its own devices, was altogether more genuinely spontaneous. In Paris there was a three-day feast, but mainly for the benefit of the National Guard. Palloy organised a post-14 July street party for ordinary Parisians. This was an improvised affair, and the beginning of a cultural breach between the official and the unofficial, a parting of the ways between ceremony and holiday that was to come to define the social reality of the 14th for the vast majority of the population. The midday banquet and the evening *bal musette* could, and did, merge as a shared embrace of revolutionary civic virtues, in this regard often drawing on older religious traditions (for example, the meal as a secular equivalent of the Eucharistic feast). But they were just as much about entertainment, a time in which, released from daily labours, the people could let their hair down.

From the point of view of those in charge of the new political order, the *Fête de la Fédération* was stage-managed, not just to contain the common people, but also to consolidate a particular version of the Revolution; as throughout the whole history of the revolutionary festival, 'memory' was to be at the disposal of one agenda or another, and the past subordinated to the perceived requirements of the present. Behind the public display of concord, the festival was designed to outflank a political adversary (already the theme of the Enemy lurking behind the veil of Fraternity) in a barely concealed contest for power over not just what the Revolution meant, but to whom it belonged. Thus the Oath, as outwardly the spectacularised confirmation of the national Pact, gathering and transcending all interests, was in fact subtended by the politics of faction and party, namely Lafayette's. Above all, 14 July 1790 was Lafayette's day, and *fayettiste* was soon to emerge as an adjective for the political settlement the festival had ratified (a constitutional monarchy). One of the first places (along with the site of the Bastille) visited by the federates arriving from the provinces was the

Tuileries, as a kind of holy site at which one might catch a glimpse of the king. The purpose of the festival itself was to protect not disturb the peace, to 'complete' the Revolution through an act that, in commemorating a beginning (14 July 1789), also marked an end; the abbé de Patry summed it up when he claimed that the festival 'puts the final seal on the most memorable of revolutions'.

There were of course dissenters, notably among the radical journalists. Desmoulins mocked the festival, with in particular a coruscating snapshot of Lafayette in strutting mode, as ego run amok, and Louis as a pathetic, humiliated wretch (on this point at least Edmund Burke agreed with Desmoulins, though naturally without sharing the latter's glee at royalty's abjection). Loustalot described the 'ensemble' of the festival as a 'beautiful' display of unanimity before, however, switching to its 'details': 'a crowd of idolators dazzled by M. Lafayette', the *Vainqueurs* ignored, not a word in memoriam for those who perished on 14 July 1789, self-prostituting leaders of the Constituent Assembly, the 'insolence' of marshals and generals putting themselves before their troops, a 'thousand ruses' to rob the citizen of all capacity to 'reflect', a moment 'poisoning' the well of memory and dedicated more to 'forgetting' than remembering. This was strong stuff (and in many respects also devastatingly right). But it was the acme of restraint alongside Marat's characteristically venomous broadsides of 16 and 18 July. In his first report, Marat described the proceedings as a brazenly 'shameful' charade mounted by a collection of fat cats bent on optimising the political conditions for lining their own purses, while betraying the true interests of the common people, broken by unemployment and hunger. The festival promoted a 'false image of public happiness' to 'distract the citizen from

public affairs' (by which more concretely he meant prevent-
ing the Parisian 'sections' from preparing for the forthcom-
ing elections). The image both masked and accentuated the
reality of a 'divided' nation. But Marat's denunciation went
one stage further, beyond the exposure of a gimcrack fabrication to the charge of 'conspiracy'. With his unique mix of
the hysterical and the lucid, he went for the political jugular
by attacking the centrepiece of the occasion, the Oath. This
was not just a confidence trick practised on the vulnerable,
but the crucial element of a 'plot' engineered by royalists and
Lafayettists to secure collective support for the 'constitution
before it has been ratified'. It was a recipe not for establish-
ing rights but for sacrificing them, not for democracy but
for 'tyranny': 'sustained by your support, if you refuse to
underwrite oppression and tyranny, they will remind you of
the oath you swore, and force you into becoming the oppres-
sors of your comrades, from fear of perjuring yourselves.'
As the voice of the *sans-culottes*, Marat had every reason for
writing: 'Why this unbridled joy? Why these evidences of
foolish liveliness? The Revolution, as yet, has been merely
a sorrowful dream for the people!' Part of the point of the
Fête de la Fédération was to declare the Revolution 'over'; for
Marat it had yet to begin. From the purely predictive point
of view, Marat won the argument, although this was something of a self-fulfilling prophecy given that he himself was
partly instrumental in bringing about what he foresaw.

⧗

This brash mix of the splendid and the tawdry, genuine
enthusiasm and cynical opportunism, was an unrepeatable
one-off. In the rich pageant of festive revolutionary festivals

to come (literally thousands of them), there were competitor festivals (perhaps the grandest and the strangest the Festival of the Supreme Being). But where 14 July is concerned, none of the successors came anywhere near matching the bravura of the first. The only muffled or discordant note, drowned out by the collective clamour of *Je jure*, was the semi-detached attitude of the king. By the following year he was fully, and permanently, detached; the oath he had uttered deemed worthless. But he was not the only historical actor to renege on a pledge solemnly given. The problem with oaths is that, however solemn and publicly ritualised, they can be betrayed, or at least their meaning varyingly interpreted. By 1791 the political landscape had changed substantially and the 1790 compact was in the process of unravelling. Whatever the construction the king had put on the constitution he swore to uphold, he had no intention of relinquishing the veto powers traditionally vested in the doctrine of divine right. In the meantime, he and the rest of the royal family had absconded, his image as Father of the People irreparably damaged by the flight to Varennes in June 1791, from where he could – though whether he intended to remains uncertain – summon the émigrés and foreign armies just across the border threatening to put an end to the still-nascent Revolution. The festival of 1790 which had promised 'closure' now stood as a hollow promise, and the 14 July celebrations were never to be the same again. If there was a large quotient of sheer fakery in the 1790 *fête*, there is still something to Kropotkin's view that it was 'one of the most beautiful popular festivals ever recorded in history' (Wordsworth, who found himself in Chalon, on a boat with a contingent of *fédérés* returning from Paris, remarked on the atmosphere of 'benevolence and blessedness spread like a fragrance').

Certainly 14 July 1791 was a beautiful day, but, along with the sun in the sky, there was also insurrection in the air, and the festival itself, if this time spared the torrential downpours of the original, was nevertheless something of a washout. The real crowd-pulling event had taken place but a few days previously: Voltaire's funeral (more accurately his secular canonisation, the transfer of his remains to the Panthéon, a former church recently converted into a resting place for the 'great men' of the nation). This was an extraordinary public consecration, the purpose of which was to appropriate the reputation of the great man for the Revolution (all very different from the time of his actual death in 1778, when newspaper obituaries were prohibited and the French Academy barred from holding the customary memorial service for deceased members). To make the point, the coffin was deposited at the ruins of the Bastille the night before the procession (the ghost of Enlightenment thus marking the spot of the fall of Despotism). The procession itself did not get to the Panthéon until around midnight the following day, the sarcophagus accompanied by members of the Constituent Assembly and the Paris Commune, and the casket inscribed with the words: 'Poet, philosopher, historian, he made a great step forward in the human spirit. He prepared us to become free.'

In a sense, therefore, the Bastille celebration had already taken place (the Bastille connection strengthened by one of Palloy's miniatures, made from the prison stones, being one of the main embellishments of the cortège). But there remained a score to settle. The king was not only personally absent from the second *Fête de la Fédération*; the ignominy of Varennes meant that all trace of his consecrated place in the national compact was expunged. The original triangular dedication on the Altar to the Fatherland had been emended: 'the Nation, the Law, the […]'. Lafayette once again hogged the limelight, but this was not to be a re-run of Lafayette's day. Suspicion and disappointment had replaced jubilation. Marat's talk of 'plots' now seemed all too plausible and his hyperbolic description of Louis ('crowned brigand, perjuror, traitor, conspirator') far more likely to find a sympathetic audience; Lafayette was doubtless much disconcerted on hearing cries of 'Down with the king' as he pranced on his white charger. The Constituent Assembly moreover sent a mere token representation and declined to suspend its sitting, one of its tasks for the day the hearing of a petition from the radical Cordeliers Club (Danton's base) calling for a referendum on the future of the king. Moderates in the Assembly managed to defuse the situation, initially 'suspending' and then reinstating Louis within the terms of the still-unratified constitution. On 16 July, however, a further petition – this time demanding the deposition of the king – was drafted, read out, from the four corners of the Altar to the Fatherland, to a large crowd gathered at the Champ de Mars and by early evening signed by over 6,000.

The following day Lafayette and Bailly, determined to put an end to these stirrings of 'popular democracy', came to the Champ de Mars with a contingent of National Guard to enforce martial law (decreed the previous evening). The crowd refused to disperse and the militia opened fire (estimates of fatalities ranging from thirteen to fifty). This – what came to be called the 'Massacre of the Champ de Mars' – was the bloodiest incident since the taking of the Bastille, this time, however, with a capital difference: the people's militia had attacked the people. The petition was subsequently lost in the fire that devoured the Hôtel de Ville in 1871 during the

Communard uprising, but is known to have included the names of many of the *Vainqueurs de la Bastille*. It seems that Danton, who read out the petition at the Champ de Mars, did not actually sign it (perhaps from considerations of prudence). As for Robespierre, while he argued in the Assembly for the immediate trial of the king, and wept copiously at the Jacobin Club for the victims of the 'massacre', he kept both the petition and the petitioners at arm's length. Yet nothing was to be the same again. The hallowed locale of collective revolutionary memory, and in particular the Altar of the Fatherland (on the steps of which many had lost their lives), were now stained with blood, and as a consequence commemorative festival was about to acquire a distinctively 'republican' aura.

The next *Fête de la Fédération* was something of an anti-climax, the day itself mattering less than the speeches and manoeuvres around it. The happily inclusive slogan 'Nation, Law and King' must by now have seemed a distant memory. Despite Varennes, Louis persisted with his claim that the royal veto was consistent with the letter and the spirit of the new constitution (finally promulgated in September 1791). In this he succeeded only in making himself even more unpopular, while, for his part, Lafayette, when not detested for his role in the Champ de Mars repression, was widely perceived as a figure of fun. The royalist cause, however tempered by liberal-constitutional nicety, was rapidly becoming a lost cause. On 20 June a demonstration was planned to protest against the king's veto powers (the date consciously chosen as the third anniversary of the Tennis Court Oath). This was to comprise a further petition (to be presented to the Assembly) and the planting of a Liberty Tree in the Tuileries garden. Once again the National Guard was summoned to disperse the crowd and once again the prospect of a further 'massacre' loomed. Although the crowd did not get to plant the tree in the garden, they did succeed in invading it. This time the militia did not fire, chiefly because their orders failed to come through, but also because the National Guard was now torn asunder, many siding with the demonstrators. The crisis was defused, but it was a foretaste of what was to happen two months later, the outcomes of which were to transform the face of festive Paris.

The domestic political temperature was further raised by the fact that France was now at war with Austria and Prussia. In early July the Assembly had issued the proclamation of *la patrie en danger*. 'Danger' was indeed now the watchword, and it presided over arrangements for 14 July. In the spring the new Legislative Assembly had delegated to the Committee of Public Instruction the task of drafting a bill for the regulation of public festivals. Shortly before, Robespierre made a speech to the Jacobin Club for a new kind of *Fête de la Fédération*. Elected detachments of the militia would gather in Paris from all over France, to swear fealty to a martial slogan: 'Liberty or Death' (the original version of the Revolution's most famous rallying cry being 'Liberté, égalité, fraternité ou la mort'). Death was now the proud, and exclusive, partner of Liberty, as Robespierre moved to his peroration: 'Come, on the tombs of our brothers let us mingle our tears and weapons, remind ourselves of the pleasures of the celestial virtues, and die tomorrow, if need be, from the blows of our common enemies.' This was a formula for a more Spartan festival, in which moreover the entire Legislative Assembly would take part (Robespierre coupled this demand with a proposal for the construction of a new Assembly building on the site of the demolished

Bastille, big enough to allow the common people to observe, and monitor, the actions of their legislators). The idea was to break once and for all with the corruptions of pomp and circumstance, in favour of an austere if overwhelming spectacle of militarised civic virtue. The speech was intended as a mobilisation against the enemy both without and within. But, in its linking of sacrifice and death to ancestor-worship (not just those who had fallen at the front or, the previous year, before the Altar of the Fatherland, but all who had martyred themselves in the cause of the Revolution), Robespierre's address also hit a truly ominous note; invoking and appeasing the spirits of the nation's dead was to become a central feature of the blood-and-soil nationalism of the far Right (although its partisans would never have dreamed of seeing Robespierre as one of their own ancestors).

It has been said that on 14 July 1792 the Champ de Mars was more like a 'military encampment' than the site of a festival. For the *fédérés* there was a circle of eighty-three tents (representing the eighty-three departments of France), in the centre a huge marquee for king and Assembly, a memorial for the war dead (Robespierre's idea) and a Tree of Feudalism adorned with various symbolic baubles representing Privilege, which the king was supposed to set on fire. The royal family sat through the whole thing in tears, with the king as ever abstracted and the crowd hostile. After reviewing the procession, he had to push his way through the crowd to swear the oath at the altar; though under military protection, there were fears for his person in the crush. He went through the motions of swearing the oath, but balked at being required to burn the tree. His authority in tatters, he was escorted at his own request to the Ecole Militaire: it was his last public appearance of this kind. In 1791 the king's name had been effaced; in 1792 it was the turn of the institution itself. Danton placed a motion before the Jacobin Club that the National Guard from the provincial departments should remain in Paris until 'liberty' had been established (now equated with the republic and the end of the monarchy). Late in July the militia contingent from Marseilles arrived belatedly, singing Rouget de Lisle's song, henceforth, by association with the singers, to be baptised and immortalised as the 'Marseillaise'. Less than two weeks later, on 10 August, came the *coup d'état*, many of the National Guard that had remained in the city marching on the Tuileries. The monarchy had come to an end, the republic was shortly to be declared, and 14 July now had a rival, 10 August.

If 1792 was the year of the 'Marseillaise', it was also, from the point of view of the federative festival, the moment of its dreary swansong, inaugurating a trajectory of decline followed in turn by a long slumber (from which it was to be aroused only in 1880). Officially both 14 July and 10 August were to be celebrated; in his curious *XVI Patriotic Commandments*, Palloy urged the case for both: 'Always preserve the memory of the days of 14 July 1789 and 10 August 1792 and pass it on to your progeny.' This, however, was a difficult mix to sustain and in practice 10 August was now to be the date that mattered. In May 1793 the Convention passed a motion to establish a 'Republican Federation of the French People'. The term 'federation' had originally been coined to evoke the principle of unanimity (Desmoulins had called it a 'sublime idea'), but in fact no one had really known what it was supposed to mean. It was a fourteenth-century word, and not to be found in any of the late seventeenth-century or eighteenth-century dictionaries, although the adjective *fédératif* occasionally appeared in discussions of the Dutch

Republic. Yet, even with its new republican inflection, 'federalist' in the context of revolutionary politics resonated in problematical ways. It was associated with the resistance of the Gironde to the Jacobin stress on the centralised state, and by June 1793 the Girondin party in the Convention had been routed, although the federalist revolts continued in the provinces (some of them brutally put down).

As for the 10 August festival, it was decided literally to superimpose it on the memorial place of 14 July. The theme was to be 'regeneration' and a Fountain of Regeneration, a female statue in the form of the Egyptian goddess Isis, was erected on the site of the Bastille. It was supposed to look as if made from stone, but was in fact a plaster fabrication; it collapsed in 1799, as, politically speaking, did so much else. In any case, the public mood showed little sign of the regenerated. The festival was regulated, seemly, and dead. There were a few improvised events beyond the control of the Convention, often held in secret, with occasional bouts of revelry, and here and there a touch of the parodic, scoffing at authority. What large-scale animation there was proved to be essentially vengeful, as when on 10 August a sizeable crowd descended on the Basilica of Saint-Denis, intent on dispersing the bones of the dead kings of France. A mere footnote, 14 July was marked by a small ceremony within the precincts of the Assembly. It was, moreover, squeezed on both sides by the death of Marat, assassinated by Charlotte Corday on the evening of the 13th and followed on the 15th and 16th by the mass viewing of his decomposing corpse in the Cordeliers church.

The years 1794–5 were, broadly, the time of the Revolution as graveyard and the graveyard of the Revolution, through the height of the Terror to 9 Thermidor (the arrest and death of Robespierre). The conditions for commemorative festival, on 14 July or any other date, had never looked bleaker. Furthermore, as the reference to 9 Thermidor indicates, there was a further complication. It was not just that 14 July now had a competitor, either coexisting with it or officially ousting it (10 August). Strictly speaking, '14 July' no longer existed as a date at all, as a consequence of the promulgation of the new republican calendar the previous October (rescinded twelve years later by Napoleon). The calendar additionally proposed a host of new days of revolutionary festivity and remembrance, most notably the five *sans-culotides*, tacked on in order to get the numbers right and respectively named Talent Day, Labour Day, Virtue Day (*fête des actions*), Rewards Day and Opinion Day. For leap years there was to be a sixth *sans-culotide*, invested with special prestige and called Day of the Revolution.

Yet, if it no longer had a calendrical existence, public consciousness of 14 July as indelibly memorable remained strong, though, in the fraught circumstances of 1794, somewhat bruised. From this point of view, in practice the old and new calendars lived side by side. However, with the guillotine operating daily, this was hardly a time for commemorative jubilation. Executions were in fact suspended for the day, but this made little difference. Paris was tense and frightened; there were sporadic banquets, but the general atmosphere was apathetic at best. Robespierre disapproved of the banquets: France cannot 'celebrate' while there are still Enemies to destroy and the true work of the revolution to complete (in reality Robespierre was probably more concerned about seditious and conspiratorial talk around the banquet table). This was all a far cry from Lafayette's calculation in 1790 that the *fête* would signal an end to a fully accomplished revolutionary project. With the fall of Robespierre later that July, the whole festival apparatus begins to wind down, with 14 July in particular poised to leave the stage, not so much with a bang as with a whimper. In 1795 a decree was issued on 10 Thermidor (the day after the anniversary of Robespierre's overthrow) stipulating that both 14 July and 10 August were to be commemorated. In respect of the former, this meant a festival for the following year, but by then the post-revolutionary regime known as the Directory had been installed, and with it came an explosion of frivolity and blasé indifference to public life. The people had lost interest in civic virtue and wanted not so much to commemorate as to party. The Directory abandoned all pretence at coherence and voted to celebrate *pêle-mêle* 14 July, 10 August and 9 Thermidor, a ragbag of contradictions sometimes politely referred to as a compromise-formation.

The underlying desire, however, was to forget rather than remember. The deputy Grelier made a speech that caught the prevailing temper:

> In evoking 14 July and 10 August, our aim is not to celebrate bloodshed and the punishment of the guilty. On the contrary, we are trying to remove them from our memory in order not to poison the pure joy that the triumph of Liberty inspires in us.

With the advent of the Consulate (the successor to the Directory), it was then but a step from extinguishing memory of the unpleasant to the extinction of memory *tout court*. As one of the three consuls, Sieyès made a couple of dutiful speeches on the importance of 14 July and 10 August. But Napoleon Bonaparte had other ideas, all geared to burying

revolutionary memory. For a few years 14 July was continued, but essentially as a means of glorifying military victories abroad. By the time he became emperor, Napoleon
decided to abolish the festival altogether, the significant date
now to be 15 August (the date of his birth). The final blow
was delivered by the plan to erect a giant elephant on the site
of the Bastille, a.k.a. the Elephant of Revolutionary Oblivion.
This may have had something to do with one of Napoleon's
many self-images (the identification with Hannibal), but no
one really knew what it was supposed to mean. In *Les Mis-
érables*, Victor Hugo put it thus:

> One knew not what it meant. It was a sort of symbol of
> sorts of the force of the people. It was gloomy, enigmatic
> and immense. It was a mysterious and mighty phantom,
> visibly standing by the side of the invisible spectre of the
> Bastille.

It was another cheapjack plaster construction and, after the
fall of Napoleon, it became the home of the city's vermin
and quietly rotted away. But with it the work of oblivion
had been more or less accomplished. Erased, suppressed
or driven into underground clandestinity, the Fourteenth of
July ceased to exist until resurrected by the Third Republic
in 1880.

6

BASTILLE DAY

In 1880 the government of the Third Republic decided that it was in the interests of both the Republic and itself to awaken the 14 July festival from its long nineteenth-century sleep. It was henceforth to be an annual event in perpetuity, legally sanctioned as both official commemoration by the state and public holiday for the general population. This was the moment of the invention of Bastille Day. The campaign to restore the festival in some form or other had been under way for the best part of a decade, notably sponsored by the radical politician Léon Gambetta and, in a series of addresses to the Institut de France, by the scholar Henri Baudrillart. As early as 1872, Gambetta had written in his newspaper, *La République française*, of the 'need' a 'free nation has of festivals', and in one of his best-known public speeches, also in 1872, called specifically for a Fourteenth of July event, on the teleological argument that all the 'decisive *journées*' of the Revolution, including 10 August and 22 September, were 'contained' in the inaugurating *journée* of 14 July. The right-wing government, recovering from the trauma of the Paris Commune uprising, did not agree. It sought to impose a nationwide interdiction on the 14 July popular banquet, though in both Paris and the Midi the ban was often ignored. That government fell in 1877.

6. *With various emblematic revolutionary figures at the prow of a boat, floating before the newly inaugurated Eiffel Tower, republican imagery joins with the wonders of technological modernity to express the marriage of 14 July and the Third Republic under the sign of 'Progress'.*

On 21 May 1880 deputy Benjamin Raspail proposed a motion, signed by sixty-four fellow deputies, that 'the Republic adopt 14 July as the day of an annual national festival'; it became law on 6 July. But if the formulation of the law was simple, the politics behind its framing were complex. The idea of a 'national' festival was explicitly billed as a 'festival of the Republic'. Yet the meaning of the term 'republic' and its relation to the legacy of the French Revolution were politically delicate issues. Just how delicate is clear from the debates, both within and outside the Assembly, that accompanied Raspail's motion. Some deputies argued that the appropriate date to be remembered was 4 August 1789 (the date of the official abolition of 'feudal' privilege), while a smaller number favoured 5 May 1789 (when the Estates-General convened at Versailles). Others maintained that 9 Thermidor (27 July 1794), the moment of Robespierre's fall, was more suitable (in order to ensure public dissociation of the 'republic' from the memory of the Terror). The lone voice of the feverishly intransigent Henri Rochefort (*L'Intransigeant* was the name of the newspaper he created) held out for 21 January 1793, the date of Louis XVI's execution and naturally went entirely unheard. What *no one* proposed was the actual date of the founding of the First Republic (22 September 1792), indelibly linked to the coup of 10 August and the September Massacres. That would have been altogether too uncomfortable, a reminder among other things of the invasion of the Tuileries, the insurrections of 1848 and, closer to home, the violent insurrection of the Paris Commune in 1871 (which had razed the Tuileries).

The agreed solution – 14 July – was, however, also problematic, not on the logical grounds that the political demands it embodied had little, if anything, to do with 'republicanism' (for the Republican parliamentarians of 1880 it sufficed that 14 July could be posited as the historic challenge of 'modernity' to feudalism, clericalism and monarchy), but because it too was, if on a much lesser scale, stained with blood. Here was a prime case of publicly ratified 'collective memory' being brought face to face with the recalcitrance of history: the deputies wanted memory to be shaped to the needs of the fully legal republic, but 14 July 1789, however you cooked the historical books, had been unambiguously illegal. The solution was to finesse the matter with the argument that the reference of '14 July' was a double one: simultaneously to the date of the storming of the Bastille (a time of strife) and to the date of the first *Fête de la Fédération* the following year (a time of reconciliation and concord). Thus emerged the prima facie odd proposal for a festival that was to celebrate not so much an event as another festival, though it could be maintained that event and symbol, action and theatre, were so closely intertwined during the Revolution itself that the borderline between the two categories was blurred. The rationale of this ingenious superimposition of the two dates was supplied in a speech by the politician-historian Henri Martin in the Senate:

> But let us not forget that behind this 14 July, when the victory of the new era over the old regime was secured by armed struggle, let us not forget that after the day of 14 July 1789 there was the day of 14 July 1790. One cannot charge the latter with having spilled a single drop of blood, of having produced the slightest degree of division in the country. It was the consecration of the unity of France. Yes, it consecrated what had been prepared by the ancient institutions of the monarchy. The latter had,

so to speak, created the body of France, and we have not
forgotten this; the Revolution, on that day, 14 July 1790,
formed, I will not say the soul of France – only God made
the soul of France – but the Revolution made France conscious of herself; it revealed to France her soul. Let us
thus recall that on this day, the most beautiful and the
purest of our history, from one end of the country to the
other, from the Pyrenees to the Alps and to the Rhine, all
Frenchmen joined hands.

Politically speaking, Martin's effort was a tour de force,
a version of the past designed to satisfy nearly all main-
stream parties: music to the ears of 'moderate' Republicans,
a generous titbit for restive monarchists (many of whom
had opposed the whole idea) and a firm repudiation of any
claim on the revolutionary past by the revolutionary Left
(there was an attempt to coopt remaining dissidents by
granting amnesty to former Communards on 11 July 1880).
The speech provided an account of the meaning of the new
national festival perfectly tailored to the requirements of a
legitimation-narrative for the Third Republic that would
be uncontaminated by contact with everything that was
unsettling and controversial about the original Republic. In
short, it represented yet another proposal to remember by
forgetting. On 14 July 1790 France may still have been more
than two years away from becoming a republic, but never
mind, it provided not so much a precise political analogue
as a vocabulary. The new *fête* was to be a resurrection of the
tropes of Resurrection ('What we celebrate today,' wrote a
contemporary journalist, 'is the resurrection of France').
  Ironically, telling the truth in the minimal sense of stick-
ing closer to the facts fell to the royalist right (in a series of

pamphlets). They opposed the idealised fairy tale (stressing, for example, the derisory yield of liberated prisoners in the storming of the Bastille), but of course not from a disinterested commitment to truthful chronicle. They had agendas of their own, and if 'fact' was mobilised to subvert fiction, it was in order to discredit the whole revolutionary enterprise. When General Ambert referred to the festival as *la fête de la désertion* (of the *gardes françaises*), he highlighted a historical truth, but missed the essential point, primarily because he wanted to identify desertion not with patriotism but with treason. Moreover, the (selective) stress on fact over fiction was no impediment to producing lurid fictions of their own: 14 July as 'madness', the 'festival of assassination' and the 'first act of the Terror', along with the storming of the Bastille as 'satanic', a scene of 'carnage and cannibalism'. The purveyors of this agitated idiom were doubtless inspired by Taine's *Origines de la France contemporaine*, the volume dealing with 1789 having been published in 1878. The upshot was that the faithful were asked to stay at home and fast, as a mark of contempt for the republican banquet. Some placed religious symbols on their balconies, in counterpoint to the republican flags which adorned the city.

The programme for the first Bastille Day comprised several elements: alms-giving to the poor, public concerts, firework displays, illuminations. The two main ceremonies were to be the presentation of colours to the troops at Longchamp, with President Jules Grévy in attendance, and the inauguration of a monument at the place de la République under the auspices of the Paris municipality. Both involved the introduction of new ritual and symbolic motifs, most importantly the flag and the statue. The military theme that had always been at the forefront of the 14 July celebrations

was now unambiguously what the state wished to emphasise most (as a way of healing the wounds inflicted by defeat
in the Franco-Prussian War). The dominant conception was
'nationalist' rather than 'republican', and its rallying point
the union of army and nation under the flag. The tricolour
became a public revolutionary emblem in 1789 when, on 17
July, Bailly, the mayor of Paris, presented a submissive Louis
with the red, white and blue cockade. The colour scheme –
which may have been Lafayette's idea – combined the red
and blue of the city's coat of arms with the traditional white
of the French monarchy. Those wedded to new conceptions
of sovereignty were inclined to see the placing of the white
band between the red and the blue as a conscious statement
of the king's subordination to the will of the people; those of
less polemical dispositions saw it rather in terms of an ecumenical embrace carrying the promise of a well-ordered constitutional monarchy. In 1794 the Convention adopted this
design when it decreed the *drapeau tricolore* as the national
flag to replace the two royal standards, the *oriflamme* and
the *fleur-de-lys*. The oriflamme (its colour flaming red and its
name from Latin *aurea flamma*, 'flame of gold') was originally
a religious banner belonging to the Basilica of Saint-Denis
(as the burial site of monarchs, it was France's equivalent
to Westminster Abbey) and, from Carolingian times, was
used only in battle (its bearer a military post of considerable honour and prestige). The white flag embroidered with
a fleur-de-lys (a symbol of purity) as the royal coat of arms,
was alleged to have been first adopted by the Frankish king
Clovis on his conversion to Christianity towards the end of
the fifth century, but it was especially associated with the
Bourbon dynasty and the doctrine of divine right. It made
a brief reappearance after the fall of Napoleon during the

Bourbon restoration and, in altogether more provocative mode, during the Vichy regime under Nazi occupation.

The politics of the flag were thus highly charged. The symbiosis of soldier and citizen was a crucial component of the revolutionary legacy, including the history of its commemoration from the first *Fête de la Fédération* onwards. The first Bastille Day took this a stage further. The flag was not confined to the official military parade at Longchamp, but was displayed across the whole city, festooning streets and buildings (an echo of the 'pastoral' festival two years previously which Monet painted as an impressionistic sea and swirl of colour). The idea was to saturate civilian life with reminders of the civic meanings of the military ethos. The running context for this was the bitter conflict between laity and Church, the principal battleground of which was in the sphere of education. The decade 1880–90 was the time when 14 July was vigorously and successfully used to prosecute the campaign of anti-clerical secularism that was the hallmark of the Third Republic's version of 'republicanism' (the final separation of Church and state occurred in 1905). The school was seen as a place of civic instruction and as a breeding ground for the production of the good citizen. The inculcation of lay-patriotic values in schoolchildren, concluded the Paris *conseil municipal*, should be one of the primary purposes of the festival ('one cannot associate them too soon with national and republican festivals'). In 1882 schoolboy battalions were included in the 14 July military procession (precedent was furnished by the children's 'battalion' in the 1790 *Fête de la Fédération*); as miniature soldiers, to whose hands the security of the fatherland would eventually be confided, the schoolboys constituted a preparatory sketch in which past (glory), present (celebration) and

future (safety) could be combined. This implicated not just
the social but also the biological reproduction of the good
citizen. The Municipal Council further stressed the importance of associating girls – the future mothers of the nation –
as well as boys with the festival: it is 'only republican women
who can make good republicans of our children'. Naturally,
the Church disagreed; its 1909 index of prohibited works
included a number of school history books, especially those
devoted to the French Revolution and specifically the events
of 14 July 1789.

The second major innovation was in the choice of a
public representation to embody the spirit of the Republic.
This was the figure of Marianne. Its origins as a political
icon are obscure. Some have maintained, a trifle implausi-
bly, that the name is a deformation of Juan de Mariana, the
sixteenth-century Jesuit who wrote a defence of tyrannicide.
Other exotic sources include an off-the-cuff improvisation
by Paul Barras during the government of the Directory (he
was one of the five executive Directors): at a dinner party
he allegedly asked the name of his hostess, the wife of his
political colleague Jean Reubell; on learning that it was Marianne, Barras is claimed to have remarked that it was a name
'which befits the Republic just as much as it does yourself,
Madame'. Serious research, however, has uncovered a more
authentically revolutionary origin in a Provençal folksong
by the poet Guillaume Lavabre, routinely sung during 1792
in the area around Toulouse, and in which Marianne represents the Republic. In September the same year the Convention decreed that the new seal of state should be marked
with a woman holding a pikestaff and sporting a Phrygian
cap, though she was not explicitly named as Marianne. She
was, however, to lead an extremely active radical afterlife,

from her appearance in Delacroix's famous picture of 1830 (*Liberty Guiding the People*), a pictorial image that was to become ubiquitous, on the back of official authorisation by the Ministry of Interior, during the short-lived Second Republic. During the Second Empire depictions of Marianne were driven underground, where they served as a clandestine symbol of opposition to the imperial regime.

The retrieval of Marianne by the Third Republic was nevertheless not uncontroversial. The Church deplored Marianne replacing Marie (on 14 July 1880 the devout placed busts of the Virgin on their balconies), while the royalist right referred to her contemptuously as 'Marie-Anne' (allegedly her original peasant name). But these were largely disgruntled noises off-stage. It was within the republican camp itself that the significant division of opinion was to be found. For, if there were to be busts and statues of Marianne publicly displayed in the town squares of republican France, what was she to wear, in particular what was her headgear to be? Revolutionary tradition had consecrated the Phrygian cap (in ancient Rome worn by emancipated slaves to mark their freedom), and the Paris municipality followed tradition when in 1879 it commissioned the statue that was to be situated at the place de la République and ceremonially unveiled on 14 July 1883. But this was not the face of the Republic that a queasy government wished to endorse (too redolent of insurrectionary *sans-culottes*, Communards and striking workers), and it asserted its preference for the alternative to the *bonnet rouge*, the more bucolic and peaceable wheatsheaf crown (the president and his government ministers stayed away from the unveiling). One barometer of tensions between 'moderate' and 'radical' republicans throughout the Third Republic is the extent to which the crowned and the bonneted, the placid and the fiery images of Marianne vied with one another. One thing that was universally agreed, however, was the adoption of the 'Marseillaise' as a national anthem.

As deputies, ministers and mayors debated meanings and bickered over symbols, what did the first Bastille Day look like from the point of view of the common people? The most widely read daily newspaper in Paris, *Le Temps*, reported that the 'whole population of all classes and all nuances took an active and joyous part'. This obviously has to be journalistic hype, but all the evidence suggests that the politically manufactured chimed with the popular mood. Other than in the Vendée region (still scarred by memories of what was claimed to have been 'genocide' – the revolutionary suppression of the royalist uprising in western France), the whole of France appears to have greeted and joined the festival with unforced alacrity. What precisely was being celebrated of course varied considerably. In Paris allusions to the storming of the Bastille were conspicuously absent. Some street vendors sold small replicas, but this was more a knick-knack trade, equivalent to the later buying of a replica Eiffel Tower from a street hawker. In the provinces, and especially in the south, the political tone was sharper. In Saumur a descendant of Aubin Bonnemère, the *Vainqueur* who had presented one of the Bastille stones to his native town – it had since been buried somewhere in the cellars of the Hôtel de Ville – campaigned successfully for it to be taken out and dusted down.

But the key to the generally amiable sociability of the 1880 festival is the fact that it was also – for the first time – a public holiday. If the 'people' was to participate fully in 'its' national festival, it had to be given a day off work, and thus republican 'memory' was joined with and expressed through a collective form of the modern leisure culture. Over time the two were to diverge so far as to leave very little felt connection between them, but in 1880 the general euphoria was such as to mask the early stirrings of that eventual rupture. Entertainments, both planned and improvised, included bonfires, fireworks, races, cockfights, *boules* and, above all, feasting and dancing (the republican *banquet* at midday and in the evening the popular *bal*). Some of the primmer advocates of republican civic programming saw the dancing as training for the body, a useful preparation for military service. But this was a truly fatuous rationale, with no purchase at all on the ordinary working people, for whom the *bal* combined ancient festive practices and sheer pleasure (in Paris the dance halls were also pick-up places, the more louche transactions of popular festival in the capital caught by some of the Impressionist painters; no surprise, then, that the conservatives described festive Paris as 'a cheap dance hall' and 'an immense orgy').

Where the political capture of the popular imagination was more successful lay not in imposing a disciplinarian blueprint on mundane pleasures, but in creating pleasures that, by their very nature, could serve the cause of social tranquillity even as a revolutionary past was being marked. This seems to have been one of the intentions behind the use of the new technologies of illumination. Illuminated Paris on 14 July 1880 was typically described in the contemporary accounts as 'féerique', the momentary conversion of the urban landscape into a kind of fairyland, offering not only a brief respite from the grindingly ugly world of daily work, but also an escape from memory itself, in which a potentially uncontrollable revolutionary heritage was replaced

by an agreeable mirage. For, along with the festive affirmation of the legitimacy of the republic against its enemies on
the Right, there was also a real fear of trouble from the Left
(the fall of the Bastille was to be celebrated as 'a definitive
victory, not as a battle to be recommenced', as one provincial newspaper put it on 18 July 1880). Especially sensitive
to recollections of, and continuing attachment to, the 1871
uprising, the government prohibited 14 July gatherings at
Père-Lachaise, where so many Communards had fallen in a
bloodbath. There was considerable anxiety over what might
erupt at local republican banquets, with fighting talk fuelled
by alcohol. There was also the worry, at a time when republic
and capital were now on exceedingly fraternal terms, that an
outburst of radical sentiments might have an adverse effect
on the stock market (the *Bourse* in fact rose the day after the
festival). Illuminated dreamlands were one way of seeking
to secure the appropriate political slumber, amusement as
less a training of the body than a seduction of the mind.

⌛

The 1880 festival created a template that, with some modi-
fications and a few wartime exceptions, has been continu-
ous. The detail of that annual self-reproduction, as basically
a saga of repetition, need not concern us here; there are, after
all, few changes one can ring to a fixed repertoire. By far
the more compelling story lies in the attempt to capture,
by way of a series of snapshots, something of the changing
circumstances and fluctuating allegiances of Bastille Day
at and around certain key historical moments, typically –
and understandably – moments of stress, convulsion and
recovered solidarity in the life of the nation. Six such spring

automatically to mind: 1889, 1899, 1919, 1935–6, 1940–42 and 1945, six dates related successively to the Second International and the new forms of worker militancy nourished by Marxism and socialism; the climax of the Dreyfus Affair; the Armistice of the First World War; the formation of the Popular Front; the Vichy regime under the Occupation; and the Liberation of 1945. In their different ways, these are the moments when the ideological fix, of which the *fête* was a major ingredient, gluing together the terms republic, nation, revolution and people, came unstuck from the pressure of internal conflicts, only to be reapplied when France faced and emerged from the external threats of two world wars. In short, the history of Bastille Day from the late nineteenth century to the end of the Second World War can be seen as a kind of prism through which to view critical moments in the social and political history of modern France.

If 14 July 1889 was the date of the centennial (a subject for the next chapter), it was also, and not by coincidence, the date of the First Congress of the Second International. From the point of view of the emergent worker and socialist movements, 14 July carried a distinctly 'red' meaning. During the 1848 insurrections the red flag was often flown, while workers in the more militant *faubourgs* defied prohibition and organised their own 14 July banquets. With the founding of France's first socialist party, the Federation of the Socialist Workers of France in 1879, the class-based struggle over the revolutionary heritage of 1789 became more visible. The issue here for the Third Republic was not the dispute between laity and Church, or the parliamentary conflict between republican and royalists (the latter, however vociferous, were clearly on the losing side of history), but the antagonism between labour and capital. In this mighty confrontation, a simple but stark question was posed by the radical Left: what, or rather who, were the republic and its symbols *for*? The revolutionary socialist Guesde, who with Marx's son-in-law, Lafargue, had founded the breakaway Parti ouvrier français in 1882, was in no doubt. The memory of the Bastille had been hijacked for the construction of a new citadel of incarceration: 'a Bastille of the capitalist class'. Two of the terms of the Revolution's great slogan, liberty and equality, were in some vital respects now enemies rather than friends (the third, fraternity, remained variously inter-pretable on a spectrum from just being nice to one another to the need for organised solidarity).

Where the state-sponsored festival itself was concerned, there were two options for the Left, reappropriation or boycott. The socialist leader Jean Jaurès supported the first option, repudiating the official association of 14 July with the theme of class concord and – while remaining careful not to advocate revolutionary violence – staking a claim to the true 'meaning' of 14 July in terms of popular rebellion (specifically the beginnings of the *sans-culotte* role in the making of the republic). For Jaurès and his followers the fes-tival was not just the formal property of the modern repub-lican state, now stamped RF, but belonged naturally to the People in a more radical and class-conscious sense of the term. Others, however, identified this as a trap and called for outright abstention (or alternatively showing up with a black flag). There was now, moreover, a rival to 14 July: the Second International, acting on a motion proposed by Raymond Lavigne, declared 1 May as International Labour Day (in commemoration of the victims of the 1886 Hay-market riot in Chicago). Although not invoked by Lavigne, there was a sort of revolutionary precedent for this: when in

October 1793 Fabre d'Eglantine presented to the Convention
his plan for a new republican calendar, it included the recommendation of a labour day to fall annually on (in the old
calendar) 19 September. Assuming anyone recalled it at all,
Fabre's innovation was not invoked, one imagines, because
it was more a proposal to celebrate work than the granting
of a day's release from it.

In 1892 the unions at Saint-Nazaire voted to 'abstain' from
14 July celebrations and 'henceforth recognise only 1 May'
as a festival date. This failed to attract widespread support,
most probably less from strong worker identification with
the official festival and more because the latter was a public
holiday. The state of course refused to establish 1 May as
a national holiday until well into the twentieth century. It
accordingly became more an occasion of protest and riot
than a festive gathering. In the United States, as a reaction
to the 1894 riots in Cleveland, Labor Day was moved to September (thus at a prudent distance from memories of the
original May troubles in Chicago). In France hostility to the
14 July ceremony on the syndicalist left became increasingly
vocal. Spouting the mantras of 1789 was but a political nar-
cotic administered to the masses, the republic's version of
the 'opium of the people'. In the early years of the twentieth century, with Clemenceau's authoritarian premiership
and his (merited) reputation as a strike-breaker through the
use of armed force (though he had previously been a committed Dreyfusard and supporter of Zola), union resistance
to 14 July found an echo in the caricatures of the anarchist
Aristide Delannoy (the heir of Daumier, he was sentenced
to a year's imprisonment because of his work). In one of
these a debauched Marianne is figured as receiving a bunch
of flowers from the bloodstained hands of Clemenceau; in

another the words 'liberty', 'equality' and 'fraternity' are illustrated in the background by three representatives of a grasping and repressive ruling class (a banker, a magistrate and an officer), the caption a homophonic play which can't be carried over in translation: '*Des mots…des maux*' ('words… evils'). There were renewed calls for 1 May to replace 14 July, and to the extent that the latter was to be observed at all, it had undergone an important mutation: for the militant workers it was more a time for *manifestation* than a time for *fête*.

The new fractiousness signalled by the First Congress in 1889 acquired another context a decade later, when in June 1899, and in the light of hitherto suppressed evidence, the Dreyfus case was reopened (only to be promptly closed again in September). This was the affair that split France in two, around the trial of the Jewish army captain Alfred Dreyfus on trumped-up charges of spying for Germany. Prior to the eruption of the Dreyfus Affair, several of the secularists of the Third Republic had stressed the superior 'civic' values of the Jewish (and Protestant) communities in denouncing the retrograde attitudes of the Catholic Church. It was possible to mobilise 14 July on the side of this campaign, most notably by recalling the impeccable pedigree of the abbé Grégoire. Few remembered that Grégoire had presided over the marathon sixty-hour Assembly session in Versailles that ran concurrently with the taking of the Bastille. Many, however, would have recalled his efforts to promote equal rights for Protestants and Jews, although today we will find both the title and some of the actual arguments of his *Essai sur la régénération physique et morale des Juifs* not a little unnerving. This, however, would be a mere antiquarian quibble alongside the virulent anti-Semitism of the

Dreyfus Affair, which crucially infected the military. While the army remained loyal to the state, much of its officer class was averse to republican values; Dreyfus was in part the scapegoat for that aversion.

In short, 14 July 1899 was something of a minefield. How could the festival sustain the fiction of a unified national family based on a sacred bond between army and people when it was the army itself that was centrally implicated in the affair (many commentators on the right, most famously the writer Maurice Barrès, touched rock bottom by arguing that national unity required that, even if innocent, Dreyfus should be found guilty)? On the day itself both Right and Left assembled to affirm the army, but for diametrically opposed reasons: the Right (especially the Ligue des Patriotes) to defend the 'honour' of the army at all costs (including the dishonourable); the Left (especially the Ligue des droits de l'Homme) to 'save' the army from those who sought to abuse and pervert the 'republican' ideals it was there to defend. Jaurès moved boldly, and controversially, to occupy the high ground of 1792; the army, he claimed, belonged to the people under 'the flag of the First Republic'. Nationalism and republicanism, which since the Revolution had been the two sides of the same coin, were now locked in mortal combat. It took a victimised Jew to open an ideological fault line that had been more or less successfully concealed for over a century. In places things turned nasty. In Rennes a group of young nationalists went on the rampage, shouting, 'Down with the Jews', and smashed the windows of Victor Basch, a prominent member of the Ligue des droits de l'Homme and a well-known Dreyfusard. The fault line, moreover, widened to reveal an even deeper fissure. If the principal bone of contention between Left and Right turned on the question where, to what and to whom the army belonged, its proper relation to the state and the rule of law, there was also a more radical anti-militarist strand of opinion, arguing that the affair was not just about a few rotten apples in an otherwise healthy institution, but implicated the whole spirit of militarism and revanchism in a way that constituted a genuine threat to democracy to itself. Unlike Jaurès, who sought to reclaim ground stolen by his political adversaries, the anti-militarists, like the syndicalists (they were often the same people), sought to transform the festival into a site of contestation. This was to happen again in the run-up to the formation of the Popular Front in 1935 (in which Victor Basch was to have a prominent role).

If the aggravated relation between Bastille Day and the Dreyfus Affair replayed some of the tensions of the 1889 festival, it was also fundamentally about something else: France and its 'others'. Anti-Semitism was the bridge joining nationalism and ethnicity, the army, the nation and the flag linked as the meeting ground for what, in right-wing circles, was increasingly called 'the good Frenchman'. This had little to do with republican 'patriotism' in the older sense, but rested more on the invocation of 'stock', blood and soil that characterised the language of Action française (itself born of the Ligue des Patriotes). This group detested the Revolution and all its works, arguing not so much for an adaptation of revolutionary memory as for its liquidation, and for the replacement of Marianne by Joan of Arc. They felt that 8 May (the date of the liberation of Orléans by Joan's army in 1429) should usurp 14 July in the commemorative calendar. The original *prise de la Bastille* had been a disaster for the nation, a conspiracy of foreign Freemasons, mainly from Germany, and the source of that 'collective tyranny' otherwise known as democracy. The modern, and true, Bastille was the 'Bastille of the Republic', run by a mongrel collection of democrats, Freemasons and Jews.

In this scheme of things the unwanted ethnic 'other' was a parasite on the body of the nation. If this was to have a place at all in the festive proceedings, it was as an exotic exhibit. The 1889 World Exhibition, timed to coincide with the centennial of 1789, had as one of its displays a 'Negro Village' in which around 400 natives were put on show in a kind of ethnological zoo. As if to make amends, in the 1950s de Gaulle invited a group of African leaders as guests at the 14 July celebrations to mark the policy of decolonisation and the creation of something called a new French Community (a kind of Commonwealth). But making amends was not so easily done. To grasp the wider history – of slavery, colonialism and racism – to which the Dreyfus episode belongs in connection with Bastille Day, it needs to be framed by both a flashback and a fast-forward. First, back to Toussaint L'Ouverture, the Haitian leader of the slave rebellion who in the late eighteenth century threw the Declaration of the Rights of Man and the Citizen back in the faces of the colonial masters. The revolutionary leaders (and later enemies) Brissotin and Robespierre had both voted in support of anti-slavery motions, but it was only after Toussaint led the slave uprising into a military alliance with Spain and Britain in the war with France that the Convention voted for full emancipation. Toussaint figured nowhere in the 14 July celebrations (until, as we shall see in the next chapter, he was, belatedly and somewhat disingenuously, wheeled on to the stage of the great 'multicultural' jamboree that was to define the bicentennial). If we then fast-forward to 14 July 1953 and the time of the Algerian War, immigrants from North Africa assembled on the place de la Nation to stage their own counter-event. It resulted in a violent confrontation with the police, with seven dead and over 100 injured.

For all the tensions and conflicts surrounding it, Bastille Day nevertheless went on to reproduce itself more or less placidly throughout what remained of the *belle-époque*. The imminence and then the outbreak of war brought a rude awakening. The agreeable times were gone, mobilisation, of both men and mood, was the order of the day. On 14 July 1913 there was a huge rally at Longchamp. Anti-militarism was a dead letter, disreputably eccentric when not flagrantly treasonable. The following year, with the nation actually at war, the Bastille found a new metaphorical incarnation: Germany, its prisoners Alsace and Lorraine. The year 1915 witnessed the attempted bracketing of the festive in the festival. The divergence of ritual and holiday into separate realms had been under way for over three decades, but the disconnect was now an embarrassment to this new incarnation of the *patrie en danger*, for which ceremony and revel could not that easily coexist. The government decreed that 14 July was to be 'exclusively patriotic and commemorative'. Street festivities were banned, partly because of blackout requirements, but also because it was felt that wartime was not party time.

The Armistice saw the return of the festive atmosphere, in one of the most extravagant 14 July *fêtes* ever. But it was primarily festivity in the service of a military achievement. In addition, 1919 saw the release of Abel Gance's film *J'accuse* (an echo of Zola's famous intervention), but this was not a time propitious to recalling the Dreyfus Affair. The army had distinguished itself, saved the Republic, and the first Bastille Day since the end of the war was to be a Victory Day. Its official themes were Victory, Right and Law, with much talk of the ancient Germanic foe, going back to the fifth-century Teutonic invasions of Gaul and the institution of feudalism. In early nineteenth-century historiography a link had been established, notably in the writings of Augustin Thierry, between an oppressed medieval Gaul and the Third Estate of 1789, generating an analogy between the Germanic warrior-barons of the early Middle Ages and the exploitation of the common people by the 'feudalism' of the *ancien régime*. Its transfer to the defeat of Germany was of course blatantly opportunistic, mere dressing for what had been a contest of nation-states, and revenge for defeat in the Franco-Prussian War. And to the extent that the French Revolution was evoked, the emphasis fell only on the first term of the expression, as something distinctively 'French' rather than revolutionary. The nation and its borders were what mattered. The autochthonous blood and soil ideology of the far right had a field day, its inspiration more the more nationalist theses of the historian Fustel de Coulanges than the liberal historiography of Thierry. There was not a trace of the Third Estate, or the insurrectionary *sans-culottes*, in any of the official discourses. All was swamped by a semi-delirious greeting of the returning soldiers, in a procession led by Marshals Joffre, Foch and Pétain. Two hundred painters were employed to produce gigantic pictures to accompany the victory parade along the stretch from the place de la Concorde to the Arc de Triomphe. Fragments of destroyed German artillery capped with the effigy of a triumphant *coq gaulois* were held aloft. There was no music, the silence finally broken by a thunderous ovation for the saviours of France. This is doubtless why Barrès recorded that on that day he was in seventh heaven.

Throughout the 1920s and the first half of the 1930s there

is little of note to report on the fortunes of the 14 July festival. Peace had restored the more peaceable forms of collective remembrance, with also a pull away from the collective to the personal, the public to the private. In 1933 René Clair's film *Quatorze juillet* struck the relevant note, as the affectingly poignant love story of a taxi driver and a flower seller against the background of the *bal musette*. Then, in 1935, a new page was turned in the modern history of the festival, a page written largely by the constellation of forces on the Left from which was to emerge, the following year, the Popular Front government headed by Léon Blum. Its text was informed by two urgently pressing questions. First, what was the point of victory in the First World War if, with the rise of fascism, Europe was hurtling towards the second? In addition, with the onset of the Stalinist purges and show trials just round the corner, what of that post-1917 phenomenon: the narrative crafted mainly by historians and intellectuals in or close to the French Communist Party (founded in 1920) which furnished both a telos to the French Revolution and a pedigree for the Russian Revolution, such that the latter could be seen as the political relative of the former and the storming of the Bastille the natural predecessor of the Potemkin mutiny (the more sceptical, however, might have reached for the Kronstadt uprising)?

The great rally organised by the Rassemblement populaire for 14 July 1935 was an attempted answer to these questions, loud and clear in connection with the first, more muted and blurred in connection with the second. There were two Bastille Days. With one significant variation, the official ceremony was business as usual, a military procession down the Champs-Elysées received by assorted politicians and functionaries. The variation was the permission to allow

Dreyfus's funeral cortège (he had died two days previously) to pass the place de la Concorde through the assembled ranks of troops, with much of the officer class presumably poker-faced; it was not until 1995 that the army officially acknowledged Dreyfus's innocence. The real event of the day, however, was the march orchestrated by the Rassemblement populaire from the place de la Bastille to the place de la Nation. It was a massive display of working-class strength and Left solidarity. Its committee president, Victor Basch, spoke on the theme of the anti-fascist cause. The communist and non-communist left buried the hatchet. Jacques Duclos, a leading figure in the French Communist Party (and in many ways a hard-core Stalinist), made a speech interpreting 'fraternité' as fraternising under two flags (albeit reserving his own as the flag of the future): 'Our enemies want to see the red flag in conflict with the tricolour, the "Marseillaise" with the "Internationale". In vain. We see in the tricolour flag a symbol of past struggles and in our red flag the symbol of future struggles and victories.' The separation of the Revolution and the Republic, much desired by the founders of the Third Republic, was now to be overcome, through the recapture of 'the great revolutionary tradition which made of 14 July a day of hope'. There was also a reprise of the public oath that had been the centrepiece of the Fête de la Fédération in 1790, now sworn to defend democracy against the threat of fascism, as well as to ensure peace and economic justice.

The following year, with the Popular Front government installed, 14 July was more a time of celebration. Once again there were two processions, but now not as rivals. The numbers were so great that two separate itineraries to the place de la Nation had to be devised. But if on 14 July 1936 the pleasures of simple festivity were recovered, it remained a *fête du peuple* in an almost lost revolutionary sense of the term 'people'. It was a day of speeches, and where there were entertainments, these were primarily directed to enhancing consciousness of a political heritage. They were reminders of a revolutionary past and its continuing obligations, the latter understood as loyalty to the Blum government, but also as the carrier of the yet unrealised promise of the Revolution. It was in many ways the exact opposite of the original Bastille Day in 1880 and the Third Republic's view of itself as the deliverer of promised outcomes in the form of its version of republican 'modernity'. To be sure, the stress fell on fulfilling the promise by non-violent and constitutional means, thus, like all its predecessors, writing out everything about 14 July 1789 that had been violent and unconstitutional. The radical journalist Albert Bayet wrote in his paper that on 14 July 1936 the 'soul of the people' had 'relived the spirit of 89', but was quick to add – enthusiastically but falsely – that the latter had been not only both 'formidable' and 'peaceable', but all the more formidable *because* peaceable. Yet the sense that something was indeed being 'relived' was palpably real, not so much a commemoration of the past as its re-enactment. Romain Rolland's play *Le Quatorze juillet* (written in 1902) was staged to full houses, its form precisely that of a living re-enactment, as if on the evening of 14 July 1936 the storming of the Bastille were taking place all over again.

In 1939 (the year of the sesquicentennial), the Popular Front was a thing of the past. As the nation moved closer to war, via the Munich settlement, Prime Minister Daladier tried to reinvoke the 'federative' example of 1790, calling the anniversary festival 'the festival of national unity', while President Lebrun spoke of 'federation' and 'defence of the fatherland'. But there were not many listening (or in attendance). By far the larger event was the procession from the place de la Bastille to the place de la Nation sponsored by the French Communist Party, its participants billed as 'the sons of the *sans-culottes* who faced the army of Coblenz' (the Hitler–Stalin pact not yet signed). Over 50,000 joined in, although – a sign that the solidarities of 1935–6 had evaporated – the Socialist Party dissociated itself from the occasion. Meanwhile, the far Right reverted to form, reminding its supporters that the appropriate image of 14 July 1789 was that of a 'pool of blood as indelible as the drops on Macbeth's [*sic*] hands'. Once again political conflict was exercising acute disintegrative pressure on the festival and its meanings. Georges Lefebvre published his great book on 1789 (*Quatre-vingt-neuf*), its conclusion an encomium to the rights of man and the citizen offered as sustenance for dark days ahead; Vichy banned the book.

The long history of *le quatorze* from 1790 to 1940 had more than its fair share of the evasive, the manipulative and the dishonest. But its one and only truly ignoble moment is to be found in that travesty of 'liberty' known as the *zone libre*, the gesture of the occupying power in 1940 towards a parodic remnant of national sovereignty. The Nazi way with 14 July was not without its own, distastefully bizarre contradictions. On 14 July 1941 the *Pariser Zeitung* published an editorial proclaiming the date as a 'significant European date' in opening a revolutionary tradition that culminated in the great twentieth-century revolution, the National Socialist one. There was also the grim coincidence that it was on 14 July 1933 that the decree of the *Gleichschaltung* banning political parties came into effect (a project that the comte d'Artois could only have dreamed of when the Estates-General convened in May 1789). The converse, and by far more influential, view was that robustly taken by Goebbels: '14 July shall be erased from history'. In the occupied zone the erasure machine went to work immediately, with a special emphasis on banning any display of the tricolour. With limited scope for resistance, ordinary Parisians fought back with resourceful cunning. Jean Guéhenno recorded in his *Journal des années noires* seeing women in Belleville wearing handmade dresses and headscarves, the resemblance of their colour scheme to the tricolour – 'of course, officer' – a mere 'coincidence'. For the more soberly dressed menfolk this was a hard act to follow; obliged to be more circumspect, they adopted the artifice of a box of matches decorated with a small illustration of the *cocarde* that protruded, at once discreetly and defiantly, from the jacket pocket.

For the Vichy regime, divesting itself of the title 'French Republic' (rebaptised the 'French State') and the motto 'Liberté, égalité, fraternité;' (replaced by 'Travail, famille, patrie'), 14 July was an encumbrance. Pétain's far-right supporters were unhappy with the whole business on any set of terms. They wanted to bury 14 July and Marianne for ever, and came up with the novel suggestion that, if there had to be commemoration, it was better dedicated to Marat's assassin, Charlotte Corday; one wonders whether any of them were familiar with Cruickshank's engraving in which Corday is depicted as Joan of Arc, the true heroine of the Right. An alternative suggestion was for celebrating the Crusades. Pétain, however, had marched with Joffre and Foch in the grand victory festival of 1919. Simply eliminating it would be a step too far. Instead of a burial ceremony, there would be the next best thing: in the words of Pétain's minister of the interior, 'a ceremony for the dead', especially dead soldiers. This was not to be a festival in the celebratory sense, but a day of mourning. Pétain himself made a speech the following year in which he defined 14 July as a time to reflect and meditate on those who had fallen in the defence of French soil. This was close in spirit to the forms of nationalist ancestor-worship favoured by the extreme right-wing movement, Action française. And, as a pointed farewell to the secularist Third Republic, the regime also brought the Catholic Church back into the proceedings, Pétain's first stop on the day being mass at the church with the archetypal crusader name, Saint-Louis de Vichy. One concession to Third Republic precedent, however, was retaining the day as a public holiday. Out of residual deference to this mockery of the 'holiday spirit' (all public festivity was strictly forbidden), the *grande rafle du Vél d'Hiv* (the biggest round-up of the Jews) was postponed until 16 July.

As at once cause and consequence of this humiliating insult delivered to republican tradition, 14 July in its more recognisable guises was claimed by the Resistance. In 1940 a brochure by de Gaulle was secretly circulated in which, predictably, the new 'Bastille' was the prison of Occupation and 14 July not a day of mourning but of recollected and renewed promise; the Resistance was the true heir of the Revolution. In his 1941 broadcast from London he declared: 'Your 14 July is not dead', and to signal that it was still alive he requested all concerned to wear the cockade. With Laval's return to the Vichy government as 'prime minister' and the end of the *zone libre* in 1942, de Gaulle issued a call to more active resistance: it was now a 'national duty' to 'demonstrate' on 14 July, wearing the tricolour and singing the 'Marseillaise'. In parts of the former free zone there was a massive turnout, along with acts of sabotage, arrests, confrontations between demonstrators and the future collaborator *milice*; in Marseille the forces of order opened fire with machine guns, leaving several dead and wounded. Laval, as the most pro-German of the Vichy politicians (it was under his premiership that Vichy would later deport Dreyfus's granddaughter to the Nazi extermination camps), was a particular focus of hatred; for every cry of 'Vive de Gaulle', there was a 'Hang Laval'. On the morning of 14 July 1942 Pétain and Laval attended a perfunctory ceremony in Vichy; afterwards over 500 people gathered and stood in silence in the town centre.

The opposite of an impotent yet resolute silence was the explosion of joy that accompanied the first 14 July after Liberation. Collective exuberance could not, however, paper over the fact that here was a nation not only exhausted but also split. First, there was the reckoning with Collaboration, and secondly, the tussle over political ownership of the Resistance. Here was the start of the scramble for domination of the post-war political landscape. The Left was already muttering that Gaullist ambitions signalled the beginnings of the 'monarchical republic', with a strong whiff of Bonapartism. The Communist Party campaigned for a sovereign constituent assembly, and to that end had organised a gathering of Resistance fighters in Paris, provocatively named the Estates-General of the Resistance. Nevertheless, 14 July 1945 was not a day for airing differences and dissensions. A huge procession of liberating troops marched from Vincennes to the place de la Bastille, where they were reviewed by de Gaulle as the new head of state. This was followed by a motorised parade from the place de la Bastille to the Arc de Triomphe. Later in the day came the celebration of the Resistance, the route now reversed, from the place de la Concorde to the place de la Bastille (thus nearly all the sacred urban spaces of 14 July commemoration were honoured). We can call this stage-managed, an attempt to rebuild the solidarities of national festival after the cracks of the 1930s and the disintegrations of the 1940s, a politically crafted recovery of the discourse and rituals of 'unanimity' that had informed the first *Fête de la Fédération*. But this account, while true at some level, also reflects the condescension of hindsight history, and completely overlooks how it was felt at the time. Where now the Marats and Loustalots who had spoken so contemptuously of the 1790 celebrations as an empty farce? Nowhere in sight.

Above all, 14 July 1945 is remembered as an ecstatic three-day street party, untrammelled release on a mass scale after the years of humiliation and deprivation. It has often been compared with the Armistice *quatorze* of 1919, for the obvious reason that both took place at war's end. But this is misleading. The latter was essentially a victory parade celebrating a feat of arms, whereas 1945 was more about deliverance, not just from the scourge of war but also from the nightmare of occupation. The restoration of 'liberty' rather than the affirmation of military prowess was its guiding theme. This is the main reason why the comparison with 1919 does not work. In the stress on liberation from an oppressor rather than victory in an external war, 1945 had a more natural affinity with 1789 than did 1919. 'Liberty', gained or regained, was the watchword (one of the largest local gatherings in Paris took place in the 19th arrondissement where an old revolutionary practice was recovered, the planting of a Liberty Tree). Liberty doubtless meant, in both 1789 and 1945, as many different things to different people as it does to the cast of characters who, in the ensemble set piece of Mozart's *Don Giovanni*, sing 'Libertà' in unison. But on the streets of Paris the unison was as much a reality as a convention or a fiction, at least in the shared affirmation of a word, if not common agreement on what it meant.

Of all the 14 July *fêtes*, there are five which stand out: 1790, 1880, 1919, 1936 and 1945. Of these, arguably the greatest was 1945, when the French people were at last freed from the long night of the worst 'Bastille' ever imposed. It is virtually impossible for historians to feel their way into the complex arc of emotions aroused and nourished by that three-day street festival – relief, sorrow, exhilaration, rapture, solemnity. It was a time when the founding trope of the founding moment – 'birth' – must have resonated in a peculiarly deep way. It was also a time when formal ceremony and festive sociability fully came together. If 1968 invented the politics of pleasure as a slogan, 1945 was a moment when the political and the pleasurable were really as one. By virtue of the presence of allied forces and diplomats, it also had an international dimension, embodying the 'universalist' thrust of Victor Hugo's line in his novel *1793*: 'the overthrow of Bastilles is the deliverance of mankind'. There had been nothing quite like it before, and there has certainly been nothing at all like it since. If Vichy represents the nadir of the Fourteenth of July, then 1945 is its zenith, after which it follows the trajectory of a prolonged, generally quiet and increasingly pale sunset, until arising, phoenix-like, from the ashes in that multicoloured confection, the bicentennial.

7. *The renowned African-American opera singer Jessye Norman appears swathed in the tricolour in front of a commemorative pedestal, to give a rendition of the 'Marseillaise'. The scene gathers together several of the motifs – an allusion to the abolition of slavery, the evocation of a trans-Atlantic conception of 'human rights' – from which the bicentennial of 14 July wove the message it wanted to project: the legacy of the Revolution as* fraternité sans frontières, *sprinkled with a dose of glitzy stardom.*

THE CENTENNIAL AND THE
BICENTENNIAL

By 1889 there had been eight Bastille Days, all of which had unfolded more or less in the intended manner, if against the background of the intensifying stand-off between labour and capital. The Third Republic appeared to have settled confidently into the ritual presentation of its own self-image as the republic of all, with no inkling of what lay on the horizon, the eruption five years later of the Dreyfus Affair. The ninth Bastille Day, however, fell into a special category, as the moment when the Day was folded into the embrace of that weightier historical unit, the Century. Yet, as it turned out, in the elaborate preparations for the centennial, 14 July did not figure as the jewel in the festive crown (in the calendar of memorable events, 14 July 1889, expressly chosen as the date of its First Congress, belongs rather to the Second International). There was a proposal from the Paris municipality to host a grand 14 July banquet, to which – in a conscious echo of the 'federation' of 1790 – all the mayors of France would be invited. While the government showed no real enthusiasm, it took place, albeit adjourned to 18 August. As for memories of the Bastille, their sole major representation was a cardboard replica built in 1888 on the avenue de Suffren.

The reasons for this partial eclipse of the 14th were not ideological, but stemmed from purely practical considerations regarding schedules. It had been decided that the centennial would be a year-long affair (celebrating 1789 as a whole), to run from late July 1888 to June 1889. In fact it did not really get under way until the spring of 1889, and moreover ran beyond the prescribed cut-off point, with the last event taking place on 21 September, the day before the legislative elections. The key date of the whole sequence was 5 May, designed to precede the real event of the centennial, the opening the next day of the Exposition Universelle. The question of which dates to mark, and which to highlight, was nevertheless a source of controversy. The indefatigable journalist and amateur scholar Charles-Louis Chassin (his name crops up everywhere in debates about the centennial) favoured a programme that would embrace 5 May, 20 June, 14 July and 4 August 1789, plus 21 September 1792. For its part, the government chose to emphasise the 'peaceable' dates, 5 May (the meeting of the Estates-General) and 4 August (the end of 'feudal' privileges). The former was declared the 'official' occasion, and included a pilgrimage to Versailles. On 20 June the Tennis Court Oath was also commemorated by a small event in Versailles, organised by the municipality, with but three ministers in attendance. Then 4 August saw the transfer to the Panthéon of the remains of Lazare Carnot, grandfather to the then President of the Third Republic, Sadi Carnot. Naturally all reference to Lazare's role on the Committee of Public Safety as the technocrat-politician who, although not centrally involved in its implementation did not oppose the Terror, was kept under wraps; in the year of the Exposition Universelle, his reputation as a mathematician, scientist and engineer probably mattered more than his standing as a player during the high period of radical Jacobinism.

The importance granted to scientific enquiry and accomplishment by the modern secular republic underwrote the two distinctive, and lasting, aspects of the centennial celebration: the archival and the monumental. In the first place, memory itself was to be given a duly scientific pedigree, through the constitution of a documentary corpus that would enable a properly 'factual' understanding of the revolutionary past. This did not of course detract from the irreducibly political character of publicly sanctioned memory, but it gave the latter a new context: the battle of the scholars, as, methodologically and institutionally, the study of the French Revolution became more and more the province of the academic profession and the specialist review. The ideological cleavage was the familiar one. In 1889 Emile Faguet – enthusiastic supporter of the Ligue des Patriotes – published his *Dix-Huitième Siècle*, a book that followed Taine's reactionary line in rubbishing the Enlightenment and its misbegotten offspring, 1789. This was part of a wider campaign by the Right reflected in a stream of brochures and pamphlets, of which the most erudite was *La Revue de la Révolution*, albeit that erudition was generally geared to the aims of propaganda.

The counter-attack was mobilised around the commanding figure of Alphonse Aulard, the first holder of the newly created chair in the history of the French Revolution at the Sorbonne, and himself centrally involved in the planning of the centennial. Intellectually, Aulard's principal adversary was Taine, his reckoning with the latter (*Taine, historien de la Révolution française*) published in 1908 as a thorough, if also polemical, critique of Taine's historical 'method', although it was not long before Aulard also had to look to his left flank, when confronted with the even more radical 'Jacobinist' historian Mathiez. Aulard's own work, mainly in the field of political history (and evincing a strongly pro-Danton bias), attracted the loyalties of a group of scholars, both within and outside the university. Its principal organ was the journal *La Révolution française*, edited by Aulard under the auspices of the Société de la Révolution française, around which was spawned, especially in the provinces, a cluster of centennial societies and committees. Supported by government funding, they produced a centennial *Histoire de la Révolution française* (also issued as a cheap 'popular' edition in instalments). The primary goal was the production of a 'scientific' historiography, but one that was also the bearer of a legitimation-story, as evidenced by the stupendous non sequitur that Charles-Louis Chassin put before the municipal commission: the 'facts established by positive method' are such as to 'prove' the 'legitimacy of the demands of our forebears'. Positivist history, in short, constructed an equation binding 'science', education, citizenship, republic and nation. The extent to which the equation could raise the temperature to boiling point is illustrated by the extraordinary incident in which someone tried to shoot Aulard after one of his lectures in the august precincts of the Sorbonne.

The constitution of the archive was thus the foundation stone of an ideological canopy designed to cover the whole nation as it prepared for the centennial celebrations. The canopy was to be further embellished by a new emphasis on the monumental. Refurbished buildings were to be political statements, most notably the Hôtel de Ville (though the huge sums devoted to cleaning it up after it had been gutted by the Communards proved controversial). But the major commemorative raids on public space took the form of what has been called 'statuomania'. Statues sprang up everywhere. The most famous was the statue of Danton, commissioned for the centennial, its inauguration, however, delayed by uncertainties over where to place it. It was finally unveiled in the Latin Quarter in 1891, but, to mark the original inspiration, the pedestal was inscribed: 'A Danton/la Ville de Paris/1889'. This was not to be interpreted as an endorsement of the violent events of 1792–3. The intended image was of Danton the 'moderate', the eventual victim of the Terror rather than one of its initiators. The more general objective, however, was simply to saturate space. Emile Bin, at once a painter and mayor of the 18th arrondissement, took this to heart with a sequence of twenty gigantic paintings depicting various revolutionary episodes and figures, which he staged as an outdoor exhibition in the Buttes-Chaumont district. The exhibition was instructively called Musée historique du Centenaire de la Révolution française, the 'museological' term an index of the attempt to bring the archival and the monumental together as partners in the Third Republic's centennial vision.

The distinctive monument was not, however, a statue or a painting, but a prodigious feat of engineering, the Eiffel Tower, itself the landmark exhibit of the Exposition Universelle. The link between the latter and the centennial anniversary was umbilical. Bureaucratically, the commissariat in charge of the Exposition was also responsible for organising the centennial programme. Symbolically, the connection of one to the other was reflected both in the schedule which arranged the opening of the exhibition for the day following the 5 May commemorative event and in the spectacular blitz which accompanied the festivities of 4 August. Carnot's inaugural speech stressed the link:

> Today France glorifies the dawn of a great century which
> has opened a new era in the history of mankind. Today
> we contemplate, in its brilliancy and in its splendour, the
> work born of this century of labour and of progress...
> She [France] has the right to be proud of herself and to
> celebrate with head erect the economic centenary, as also
> the political centenary, of 1889.

The governing idea was the republic as the natural home
of a technological avant-garde, the grand Machinery Hall
and the Eiffel Tower as the embodiment of a modernising
rationality, in contrast to the Bastille, now defined as 'medieval'. The retrospective view was cast entirely on a prospec-
tive grid. The commission turned down the proposal for an
actual Museum of the Revolution as too backwards-looking.
It was similarly unenthusiastic about the attempted resurrection of the *Fédération* festival (the proposal for a mayors'
banquet). The buzzword was 'progress', the principal set
piece a Fountain of Progress, designed by Jules Coutan and
placed on an axis linking the Central Dome and the Eiffel
Tower. It is doubtful that anyone heard an echo of the Jacobin
'Fountain of Regeneration'. This was less about the purifying
power of water than about the transforming power of electricity, a technically accomplished trumpeting of Technique
and its material benefits. The electric lights, illuminating
the entire 228 acres of the Exposition, converted the entire
site into a fairground image of Paris as the *ville lumière*. The
Eiffel Tower was dotted with enamel panels coloured red,
white and blue, lit up at night as the tricolour writ large. If
the illuminations of 1880 had for a brief moment made over
the city into fairyland, by 1889 this had become an explicit
iconographic motif: the most popular print produced for the

occasion was Jules Chéret's poster 'The Land of the Fairies –
The Enchanted Garden'.

Placing the centennial under the aegis of the Exposition
Universelle thus meant that it was less about the claims of
the past than about the priorities of the present and the pos-
sibilities of the future. It also consequentially meant that
what was being commemorated and what was being fêted
were distinct objects. The centennial was, as one commentator has aptly observed, less an anniversary of 1789 than a
paean to the nineteenth century, of which 1889 was both a
culmination and a spearhead of the future. It was in fact the
first time that the notions of 'commemoration' and 'celebration' started to diverge, the latter more the Third Republic
acting as cheerleader to itself. Naturally the Republic called
on its citizens to salute 1789, as the historic launch pad for
the process that had yielded the power and prosperity of
the last decades of the nineteenth century and beyond. But
this was to respect the past while insisting that it stay put.
The Modern had arrived as if by natural selection. Darwin's
theory indeed figured as one of the exhibits in the science
section of the fair. It was not difficult to catch the hint of a
political analogue: successfully managed adaptive change
had secured the survival of the fittest in the sense not only
of the scientifically and technologically advanced, but also
of the regime most fit to rule. If the Revolution had been
midwife to the child, the child was now a fully mature adult
who had long since flown the nest. Enough was enough.

Enchanting the collective gaze with spectacularised
representations of industrial modernity was in part a way
of disenchanting, or at least discouraging, revolutionary
thoughts. Revolutionary icons were expressly banned from
the fairgrounds of the Exposition, and few, including possibly

members of the government, would have counted the 1,792 steps of the Eiffel Tower (the illuminated tricolour by now essentially non-controversial). For, while basking in the glow of the image it had forged both of and for itself, the Third Republic was also looking anxiously over its shoulder. The cause for concern was not so much the agitations around the Second International (much of which had declared itself to be 'moderate' and 'parliamentarian'), or even the anarchist groups (in 1889 Emile Pouget started his anarchist paper *Père Peinard*, which was explicitly modelled on Hébert's incendiary revolutionary paper *Père Duchesne*). Perhaps a spectre was still haunting Europe, but it was almost twenty years since the Paris Commune, and there was little that could not be handled by a robust policing operation.

The real worry was over the possibility of insurrection and *coup d'état* under the auspices of the right-wing populist movement known as Boulangism. Hero to the army, expert in manipulating the revanchist mood (he was nicknamed 'General Revanche'), supporter of the Ligue des Patriotes, opportunistic player on the political chequerboard as simultaneously or successively conservative republican, neo-royalist and ultra-Bonapartist, General Boulanger had become a force in the land. For a moment early in 1889, he looked like being able to mobilise the resentments of the disaffected 'little man' behind a coup. By April the plot – if that is what it was – had fallen apart; Boulanger fled to Belgium, where two years later he blew his brains out over the grave of his mistress.

Several historians have suggested that one reason the plan failed was because the public mood was already entranced by the imminent opening of the Enchanted Garden. The magic worked, not only by virtue of its seductive power over the imagination, but also for the more practical economic reason that the commercial payoff in terms of tourism, exports and increased employment was considerable. It worked, moreover, not just in defusing the Boulangist threat, but also in the longer-run. There were still to be revolutionary movements and conspirators plotting coups. But these were essentially splinter formations, fractions of the body politic. There were to be no more revolutions in France. The centennial said thank you to 1789, but it also said goodbye to all that.

In certain respects the shadow of the centennial fell over its younger sister: 1889 had brought commemoration into contact with commerce not merely by linking it to but subsuming it under the Exposition Universelle. For the bicentennial, President Mitterrand wanted a repeat, and in this he was strongly supported by business leaders with an eye to the establishment of the single European market. There was also the small matter of the G7 economic summit, cleverly timed to open on 15 July, thus securing the presence of world leaders, several of whom (crucially Margaret Thatcher) were not notably fans of 1789. What better showcase for the view that France was now more about making money than about making revolutions? These, however, were recessionary times and the prospect of longer-term profits was outweighed by the immediate burden of cost. Jacques Chirac, mayor of Paris, prime minister during the period of 'cohabitation', and in 1988 failed contender for the presidential crown, effectively vetoed the proposal, albeit on grounds as much political as economic.

In the process Chirac made his own substantial

contribution to overdosing collective memory with the char-
latanesque. While as prime minister he refused, allegedly for
budgetary reasons, funding for an Exposition Universelle,
the would-be and future president of the French Republic,
in a bid for the conservative vote, had already floated the
impressively quixotic idea of a counter-festival to celebrate
in 1987 the thousandth anniversary of the French monarchy
(987 the beginning of the Capetian dynasty). Money, in its
symbolic form, was to be part of this enterprise (the government authorised the issue of a ten-franc piece stamped
with the fleur-de-lys). The best Mitterrand could manage in
terms of his European aspirations was the secular canonisation of Jean Monnet, the founder of the EEC, whose remains
were transferred by presidential order to the Panthéon. But,
if there was to be no new Exposition, there was always the
legacy of the old, especially the Eiffel Tower. The bicentennial of the Revolution and the centennial of the tower were
notionally married in a music and fireworks spectacular
(lasting of course exactly eighty-nine minutes), although
Mayor Chirac – the tower being municipal property and its
festival therefore the domain of the Hôtel de Ville – went out
of his way to ensure their divorce. And to match further the
monumentalising energies of the Third Republic, there was
the inauguration of that ultra-modern building the Arche de
la Défense on a stunning visual axis running west from the
place de la Concorde and the Arc de Triomphe; the new business quarter (uncharitably, but not unreasonably, described
as a 'business slum' and as the most anti-Paris place in Paris)
was now tied into the commemorative fabric of the city.

   This was not simply wilful vulgarisation and exploitation, but a token of shrinking options. For what in the late
twentieth century did France now have to say to itself about

its revolutionary past? What did it want to remember? How to reinvent, on an appropriately grandiose scale, an occasion that for nearly half a century had progressively ossified, the life drained from it? The last truly great 14 July festival had taken place in 1945. Throughout the Fourth and Fifth Republics, despite the ongoing conflicts between Gaullists and communists, the *fête* had become little more than a cardboard cutout, the only new addition the display of missiles to signal France's accession to the nuclear club. By the 1960s it was essentially moribund. Not even the riots of 1968, with parts of the capital barricaded, disturbed much. Largely unruffled, 14 July proceeded in its stately way, but on gammy legs and tired feet.

Take the case of 1974, on the presidential watch of Valéry Giscard d'Estaing, when 'feet' became an explicit topos under the aegis of practical reason. Giscard declared it was time for the festival to be 'reborn'. As an inclusive gesture designed to flatter what was left of the Left, it was decided that the military parade should proceed from the place de la Bastille to the place de la République. It would, however, have been a mistake to see in this an invitation to scale the heights of revolutionary memory. In a newspaper interview outlining his 'vision', Giscard contrived what was, so to speak, a remarkably flat-footed recommendation. If the festival was dying on its feet, the way to bring it back to life was by putting a newly invigorated step into the feet themselves. He thus determined that, since the storming of the Bastille had taken place on foot ('*à pied*'), the military review would take place likewise (no cars, no tanks), adding to this view of historical symmetry the eminently practical thought that 'the savings in petrol would be far from negligible' (it was the time of the oil crisis). This may have been a politically astute way of making a point to the modern 'consumer', but hardly counts as inspired. Even the French Communist Party seemed to have given up the ghost. In connection with the festival for the following year, the best its newspaper, *L'Humanité*, could muster was a limp proposition that could have come from virtually any source in the centre ground of French politics, on both the left and the right: 'the festival is a way of celebrating liberty'. By 1983 the only illustration the conservative paper *Le Figaro* could come up with to mark the festival was an image of Launay's head on a pike, accompanied by an article suggesting that 14 July 1789 had been a minor, as well as an unpleasant, event, quite unworthy of the historical myth it had been required to sustain.

These were the symptoms of a heritage grown arthritic, not to say threatened with terminal senility. It certainly meant that by the time of the bicentennial the cultural materials and political atmosphere to hand were somewhat threadbare. This, however, was no impediment to inflated expectation. They do these things differently in France of course, but perhaps only Jack Lang, Minister of Culture (also nominated, for the duration, Minister of the Bicentennial), could have pulled off this hyperbolic flight of fancy as the core of his mission statement:

In Paris, on this symbolic night of 14 July, a night of fervour and of joy, at the foot of the timeless obelisk, in this place de la Concorde that has never been worthier of the name...a great and immense voice...will cast to the four winds of history the song expressing the ideals of the 500 Marseillais of 1792.

One thing left unsaid in this uplifting dithyramb was the

fact that the 'Marseillaise' originated as a war song (a.k.a. 'Chant de guerre de l'armée du Rhin'), composed by the army engineer Rouget de Lisle while posted in Strasbourg to send off the army to fight the foreign enemy on the eastern front. What was also left unsaid was that the 500 *fédérés* from Marseilles who had arrived too late for 14 July 1792 were instrumental in overthrowing the monarchy. At first sight Lang seemed to be implying a bold commemorative move: the important date was not 14 July 1789 but the date of the coup, 10 August 1792. Not since 1793–4 had such a suggestion been floated; 10 August was strictly taboo. Was Lang lifting a nearly 200-year blanket of silence to propose that France celebrate the act which preceded and made possible the formal declaration of the republic in September 1792? It is highly doubtful that this was the intention, but, even if it was, it was a message strangled at birth. Nowhere in his hymn of praise to the Marseillaise and the marching Marseillais was 10 August mentioned. This indeed was unsurprising given the view enunciated by Prime Minister Michel Rocard of the 'meaning' of the bicentennial: 'it convinced a lot of people that revolution is dangerous and that if one can do without it, so much the better' – all too true, but not quite the point of a commemorative event focused on what after all *was* a revolution.

The lead spot for the rendition of the 'Marseillaise' was not given to anyone from Marseilles, but to Jessye Norman, who naturally converted a robustly menacing anthem into a lovely aria, delivered with professionally exquisite precision; it led one disenchanted wit to suggest that the ideal venue for the *soirée* was the place de l'Opéra, presumably overlooking the irony that on 12 July 1789 the crowd forced the closure of the Opéra. But the point of enlisting

Norman's services was not just her status as an internationally renowned singer. It was also because she was an African-American, a descendant of slaves and a focal point for a commemorative arch stretching across the Atlantic to the United States. To a large extent this was President Mitterrand's doing. The Fox played a long game, trimming his sails to shifts in the prevailing winds as the preparations unfolded. But on one fundamental point he was admirably consistent and forthright: there was a commemorative object and it was, warts and all, the French Revolution. Perhaps his finest moment was when he appeared before a gathering of historians at loggerheads and told them bluntly that commemoration meant taking the Revolution 'en bloc', the rough with the smooth (although he later adjusted this bold position to a less controversial one by saying that what he actually meant was taking the *legacy* of the Revolution en bloc rather than the thing itself). Certainly when push came to shove, the basic message he wanted sent out was the one all could rally round (apart from those for whom the Revolution was, under any description, an irredeemable abomination): the Revolution as cradle of human rights.

The truly important date, therefore, was 26 August 1789, a date that so far had not found a place in the official commemorative calendar: namely, the moment of the Declaration. But this, it will be recalled (it wasn't much recalled during the bicentennial), was a declaration of the rights not just of 'man', but also of the 'citizen'. Three years before the formal promulgation of the Republic there was here already the whiff of a republican conception, although what a republic of citizens was to mean became one of the most violently contested issues of the Revolution itself. While Mitterrand made it clear that the foregrounding of human rights was intended to echo the Declaration, the expression 'of the Citizen' was nevertheless on the whole left quietly to one side. The implicit idea seems to have been to align the legacy of the Revolution with the juridical basis of European and transatlantic conceptions of rights. The choice of Jessye Norman to sing the 'Marseillaise' evoked a link with the American Bill of Rights and also the abolition of slavery (although the Bill of Rights had evaded the slavery question). But the distinctive feature of the French Revolution which sought to tie the law-based rights of individuals to the political rights of the citizen was either buried or blurred. Once again, memory was tailored to the needs of the present. It was thus no accident that, in the protracted and intense discussions of whether it was right to mark the two hundredth anniversary of the Revolution by selectively picking out the 'good' bits and discarding the 'bad', and, if so, which bits qualified as good and bad, the recurrent figures of speech were those of the supermarket and the butcher's shop, in which the consumer hunts for the best bargains and the choicest cuts. The *Nouvel Observateur* described the theme of human rights as prime sirloin; the stakes seemed to have become indistinguishable from their homophonous partner, presumably accompanied by a portion of *frites* and washed down with a bottle of *rouge* (Marcel Amont's popular song of 1972, '*Bleu, blanc, rouge et des frites*', was dusted down for the occasion). The steaks might be served with a touch of radical garnish, but were to be dextrously trimmed of excess republican fat before being popped on the grill.

In so far as the notion of citizenship survived, it was as the cosmopolitan idea of the citizen of the world, and hence the legacy of 1789 as the universal reach of (a liberal version of) human rights in the age of multiculturalism and globalisation.

This was how Jean-Noël Jeanneney, appointed president of the bicentennial commission, interpreted Mitterrand's brief. Jeanneney found himself in a tight spot, caught between the pressure of schedules and the manoeuvres of politics. His predecessor in the post, that expert prowler of the corridors of power Edgar Faure, died in 1988 and bequeathed what by any standards was a somewhat exiguous dossier. His own signal contribution was the counter-factual thought that there were two individuals who could have prevented the Revolution from taking place at all, Turgot (about whom Faure had written a book) and himself, the thought further deepened by the observation that, alas, Turgot had died too early and he, Faure, had been born too late. Jeanneney adopted what looked like a crisper approach, characterised in some quarters as evincing a muscular 'Jacobinism', with much talk of 'civic virtue' and the like, although it would be profoundly mistaken to construe the patrician Jeanneney as a closet Robespierrist. To his credit he tried to rescue the bicentennial from a soporific consensualism based on the heart-warming incantation of 'droidlomism' (the rap version of, and comment on, *droits de l'homme*). Yet the universal and cosmopolitan framework of human rights was exactly what was needed in respect of another self-denying ordinance: 'Let us guard against all forms of Gallocentrism.' This was all very well if intended as a warning against tub-thumping nationalism, but it immediately raised a dual question: what could it mean for France to commemorate a *revolution* and what could it mean for France to commemorate *its* Revolution?

What Jeanneney came up with was, minimally, weird and, maximally, disingenuous. The commemoration would highlight four 'representative' figures: Condorcet, Grégoire,

Monge and Toussaint L'Ouverture. The choice of Monge, the renowned mathematician who had helped with the calculations involved in devising the new republican calendar, was non-controversial (an echo of the foregrounding of Carnot by the centennial as the embodiment of scientific enlightenment). The abbé Grégoire was selected as standing for 'equality', notwithstanding the fact that his conception of citizenship emphasised republican sameness rather than multicultural difference (an emphasis translated into practice through his concerted effort to stamp out regional patois and dialects in favour of a uniformly imposed common language). Nothing was made of his speech to the Convention on 21 September 1792 in which he famously argued that 'kings are in the moral order what monsters are in the natural'. As for the token inclusion of the leader of the Haitian slave rebellion, Toussaint, perhaps the least said the better. No amount of African-American operatic cosmetics could disguise the fact that Jeanneney was being a trifle economical with the *actualité*. The uprising of 22 August 1791 galvanised the Assembly into rescinding the rights of free blacks and mulattos (the slaves themselves not figuring anywhere on the political radar screen), the consequence of which was the burning of plantations and the murder of white masters. And, in addition to editing an intractable past, there was also an awkward present. A group of poor nations (including Haiti) organised a meeting in Paris to coincide with and protest against the rich man's club represented by the G7 meeting. More generally, the notionally global template of the whole affair did not in practice prove to be open house. Later the president's wife, Danielle Mitterrand, confessed to her fury at the exclusion of certain – unnamed but readily identifiable – Latin American nations on the grounds that this would have been displeasing to the United States (pulling no punches, she described it as 'shameful').

The figure in the quartet who carried the greatest weight, however, was Condorcet, the 'good' Girondin, spokesman for the 'rationality' of the market and champion of human rights (he was an admirer of the American Constitution and Bill of Rights). As the jewel in the crown, Condorcet was to be given his rightful place in the Panthéon (in the form of a plaque, his remains having disappeared without trace at the time of his death while imprisoned during the Terror). But then what of those ultimately responsible for his imprisonment and death, Robespierre and Saint-Just? Their role in the Terror and the infamous Law of Suspects was hardly an advertisement for a liberal conception of human rights. But it was Robespierre who, in his last speech to the Convention, as his support crumbled around him, said: 'The French Revolution is the first to have been founded on the rights of humanity and the principles of justice.' For his part, Saint-Just, on the day of his execution, saw hanging in the hall of the Conciergerie prison the tables of the Rights of Man and allegedly proclaimed: 'After all it was I who did that.' This may have been – to put it mildly – a claim misplaced, but, however unpalatable, the complex relation of belief and practice to the discourse of human rights that characterises Robespierre and Saint-Just would have to be part of any commemorative picture that, as Jeanneney put it in one of his braver moments, would respect the 'virulence' of the Revolution and avoid a false unanimity based on taking the 'lowest common denominator'. These brave words would be merely warm words if they did not extend to the inclusion of the Revolution's most controversial figures. But in the end this was simply too divisive. Since the Jacobin leaders were bad news, they were to be no news at all, written out of the scenario for what was to remain a comfort zone untroubled by 'virulence'. Robespierre appears to have figured but once in the history of the 14 July festival, on a poster at the great rally of the Popular Front in 1936.

Jeanneney's mission was basically a hopeless one. While demanding a certain autonomy, he had to remain sensitive to the sinuous moves of his political masters, cope with inter-ministerial rivalries, not to mention the obstructions of the arch rival ensconced in the Hôtel de Ville, Mayor Jacques Chirac. At the same time he had to plan and deliver a range of actual events. In one of his interviews he spoke of his determination to give the festival 'a clear civic meaning'. Yet, for all his intelligence and dynamism, clarity was the very last thing he produced. In the end, and despite his own warnings against tendentious cherry-picking, he capitulated: 'Let everyone take from it what they want.' This laissez-faire, anything-goes attitude was probably born of desperation before the dwindling chances of salvaging a moderately coherent programme. But it was just as much a reflection of the fact that none of this really *mattered*. For the real objective was to produce a variant of the Greatest Show on Earth, a multicultural image-fest MTV style.

In one fundamental respect the bicentennial outstripped the centennial. It did not merely juxtapose commemoration and commerce, it succeeded in commercialising commemoration itself, through the figure of the advertising whiz kid Jean-Paul Goude, whose first reaction to being asked if a bicentennial commission might interest him was the quintessential expression of postmodern cool: 'Why not?' Goude was a gifted maker of commercials with – crucially important – an instinctive understanding of the mass appeal of television (more ominously he was an admirer of Leni Riefen-stahl's filming of the Nuremberg Rally). Goude was more Lang's man than Jeanneney's, in some respects a pawn in the low-level power struggle between the two. Nevertheless, Jeanneney, a specialist in 'media history', appears to have found collaboration easy ('We worked closely and harmoni-ously with Goude and his people') and made his intention clear: the 14 July festival was to be a 'media-performance in top gear' that would 'respond to the aspirations of a con-temporary sensibility' in a manner linking 'the syncretic message' of contemporary 'world music' to 'the near-uni-versal adherence today to the message of 1789'. The nature of the link was far from clear, in particular what relation it bore to all the well-meaning talk of 'civic virtue' and revolu-tionary aspiration. The formula now was to be what works is what sells. Farewell to the *carmagnole* and hello to the pul-sating Afro-rhythms favoured by the Goude style, notwith-standing Goude's murkily exploitative relation to 'blackness' (blackness and 'animality' was one of his favourite tropes).

Goude was a truly inspired choice for the times. He can-didly acknowledged that 'in the terms of show biz' (i.e. his terms), the 'Revolution...is something that is very hard to represent'. Indeed it was, a difficulty aggravated by the fact that Goude knew next to nothing about, and showed very little interest in, the history of the Revolution. The best he could manage was the official mantra: 'For me, it's first and foremost human rights. The rest is just memory'. For the purposes of commemoration, memory had oddly ceased to count for much. What counted was what could be counted, with the foot: 'I wanted the whole of France to tap with its foot, as if in a club,' Goude proclaimed. He didn't have the Jacobin or Cordelier Clubs in mind. There was of course that last refuge of antiseptic indifference to the past, postmodern irony (Warhol was Goude's role model). 'Parody' was a term that crossed Goude's lips often as he spoke of his conception, but, since this was unlikely to recommend itself to his masters, what emerged, with a few visual jokes thrown in, was the governing theme of 'fraternity' on a planetary scale and 'revolution' defined as 'the birth of a global sound', the hybrid mixtures of world music.

The show, named for form's sake 'The Marseillaise', is virtually indescribable: that is to say, indescribably awful, a procession of floats, tableaux and images for the age of the *société du spectacle*. Only a Flaubert in unusually caustic mood could have done justice to it – a vast extravaganza of cultural and musical clichés tossed into a high-temperature melting pot, in which the melt succeeded in reducing to ashes anything intelligibly resembling commemoration of the French Revolution. Its notional openness to multiple cultures (*fraternité sans frontières*) was belied by the predominating representation of the five countries with a history of revolution (France, Britain, Russia, China and the United States) that happened also to be the five permanent members of the UN Security Council. Black Africa and little chunks of Islam were thrown into the pot, but tricolourised by projector light, which led some to wonder, with good reason, exactly what message was being projected. Toussaint of course was nowhere in sight, perhaps from sensitivity to the advice Goude, in an interview, claimed he had received from Jacques Attali: '"Some blacks, by all means, but not too many." He was right.'

The media swooned, somewhere over the moon (perhaps inspired by the Michael Jackson 'moonwalk' routine that had been the centrepiece of the finale provided by the contingent

from Florida). Hard-core voices from the left mellowed overnight, rushing to sign up for membership of the Goude fan
club. Those who remained obdurately sceptical were chided
by Jeanneney, who, now abandoning his earlier insistence
on at least an element of intellectual seriousness, reminded
all and sundry that the commercial was a legitimate art form
in its own right and that the hostility of the intelligentsia to
the advertising world was an 'old refrain' to which no one in
their right mind would pay any attention. The sole reserva-
tion President Mitterrand allowed himself was the remark
that it had perhaps 'dragged on' a bit (presumably mindful
that the taxing demands of the G7 summit called for early
nights). And that was that, the *jour de gloire* as animated fresco
of 'clips' vanishing in a puff of smoke and leaving behind
no trace apart from the bills to be settled (Goude remaining
steadfastly coy about the size of his own fee). Jacques-Louis
David had acted as pageant master to the later revolutionary festivals, including the most fraudulently meretricious
among them. But, as an artist, he had also transformed and
revitalised the pictorial vocabulary of European history
painting. By contrast, the centennial got Jules Chéret and the
bicentennial got Jean-Paul Goude.

So, what did this glitzy show really amount to? Was there
any point to it at all? Was anything being 'remembered'?
Had the tocsin of 1789 given way to its death knell? At a far
remove from the world of show business, but with a canny
eye to the value of media exposure, came a devastating
reply. Enter stage right the with-us-or-against-us, winner-
takes-all guru of 'revisionism', hailed by some as 'the king
of the bicentennial', the distinguished historian François
Furet. The intellectual and professional complexities of the
historiographical disputes preceding and surrounding the

anniversary far exceed the brief of this short book. Furet's contribution bears mentioning because of its effort to occupy not only the citadel of the historians but also the wider public sphere, as a ruthless, even pitiless, campaign to sabotage the celebratory aspect of the commemoration in terms far more sophisticated than those of the traditional counter-revolutionary right. One of the thousands of publications timed to coincide with the bicentennial was the *Dictionnaire de la Révolution française* compiled by Furet and his colleague Mona Ozouf. This was the culmination of what previously, down from the historians' version of Mount Sinai and reaching for the regal performative, Furet had proclaimed the Revolution to be: 'over'. What primarily he meant by this was certain ways of thinking and talking about the Revolution and its legacy, first and foremost the domination of memory and historical scholarship by the Jacobin tradition which, in various guises, had run from Aulard through Mathiez to Lefebvre and Soboul, inflected en route by the experience of the Russian Revolution and the prestige of Marxism on the French Left (a great deal of Furet's take was comprehensible only as a settling of scores with his own past as a member of the French Communist Party).

More radically, however, it was 'over' in that there was no longer *any* place for affectively charged memory and interpretation of the Revolution in a nation that had finally learned the difference between the 'democratic idea' and the 'revolutionary idea', critically the lesson that the former had little to do with the latter's experiment in 'popular sovereignty'; although when the going got tough Furet was prepared to concede that 1789 could be said to have provided a historical impetus for the birth of democracy, albeit in a manner pre-programmed to devour its own offspring.

Pacified and normalised, the modern French republic – the 'republic of the centre' – required an end to the interminable rehashing of the 'meaning' of the Revolution. The time had come to call time on the 'debate' itself. In 1868 the polymathic roving ambassador of French intellectual life, Edgar Quinet, remarked of the main actors of the French Revolution: 'However dead they may be for us, they are still in the fray. They go on fighting and hating.' Quinet meant of course the battles fought on their behalf in the nineteenth-century aftermath. He found this puzzling. Furet, himself a great admirer of Quinet, considered it pointless. Also baptised the 'pope of revolutionary studies', he issued the equivalent of a papal bull instructing the sectarians to stop squabbling over what by now was a non-issue.

Furet's was in many ways an odd demand for an end to the 'civil war' (as he put it) of interpretations on the matter of the Revolution. It was essentially an appeal backed by an act of intellectual *force majeure*, stipulating armistice on Furet's terms. The irony, not lost on several commentators, was that, in seeking to clear the decks and shut up shop, the militant anti-communist came to resemble nothing so much as his Stalinist adversary in effectively aiming at a 'purge'. There were to be simultaneously both no more words and a last word (Furet's own), suitably refined by the band of disciples, acolytes and collaborators that came to be known as the 'galaxy', but itself fundamentally immune to historical reflexiveness over its own status as a product of the final spasm of the Cold War (November 1989 saw the fall of the Berlin Wall). From the point of view of a pluralist culture of 'debate', this looked more like an ominous restoration of (historiographical) divine right than a further expansion of the democratic 'marketplace of ideas'. After all, and however one orchestrated the story, kings, including a 'king of the bicentennial', were not supposed to be part of it. In the immediately ambient surroundings – the world of historians, writers, intellectuals, journalists – the imperious call, though influential, happily went unheeded, and everyone carried on quarrelling. In respect of the bicentennial programme itself, Furet at least acted consistently, if a trifle churlishly. King François, while gladly accepting his crown ('I won,' he triumphantly declared to the Spanish newspaper *El Pais*), did what by his lights was the decent thing, relating to the bicentennial jamboree as a committed refusenik: 'Let's not play with words: at this point the bicentennial of 1789 seems to us the shroud of tradition.'

Quite phenomenal amounts of high-grade intellectual energy went into these disputes. Yet, when seen in the broader national perspective, the jousting amounted to little more than shadow-boxing, so much sound and fury signifying nothing. As he looked down from his position of Olympian hauteur, the self-absenting monarch could not have been entirely displeased by the ideological tone of the bicentennial. Despite his (grotesque) fulminations against the governing socialists as the heirs to the Jacobin heresy, it was broadly, if unavowedly, on Furet's terms that the wider commemoration took place – the market, individual rights, liberty as the play of private interests – in short, the panoply of liberalism. While one revolution with which the French variant had long been associated was receiving its burial rites – namely, the Bolshevik one – another from a faraway place had come, tacitly but ubiquitously, to take up abode in the commemorative consciousness: the American one (although, towed along by the undercurrents of the revision-ist wave, the English revolution also got a good billing; the nationalist gesture of Maggie Thatcher, who tried to handbag the proceedings by invoking Magna Carta, was of course a huffing and puffing sideshow). But the date that really mattered now was not 14 July 1789, and still less October 1917, but 4 July 1776. Tocqueville had prevailed over Marx, with Lafayette rising from the grave to applaud the new ideological arrangements as a reprise of the 1790 *Fête de la Fédération*, minus the military bravura and the oath-swearing ceremony at the Altar of the Fatherland. Furet may have pretended not to be listening, or have continued, perversely, to insist that Mitterrand's men were singing from a different song sheet, but this must have been music to his ears.

Yet in an important sense, diagnostically if not prescriptively, Furet was right, though in ways that he himself did not quite have in mind. The historians could continue quarrelling for ever, but where 'memory' in its more collective and diffuse forms was concerned, the game was up, 'over' in the more dismal sense of general indifference to the debate, to *any* debate, whatever its terms. Even Michel Vovelle, the historian tasked by the Ministry of Research with breathing new life into the scholarly dimension of the bicentennial, had his doubts. Notwithstanding his own strong political convictions (as an active member of the French Communist Party), Vovelle made every effort to sustain a sane dialogue between the warring parties. He grasped that what was 'good' about the 'legacy' was its unvarnished truth, the truth that so many wanted to obliterate beneath either a funeral shroud or a pastel-tinted layer of red, white and blue: namely, the fact that 'memory' and opinion were divided. He was perfectly happy for the conflict of interpretations to continue, provided it was articulated in accordance with the protocols of scholarly exchange and in the spirit of a commemoration.

Alongside Vovelle's even-handedness, Furet ultimately comes across as a mix of shabby publicity seeker, petulant diva and aggressive power broker (naturally he boycotted the international conference organised by Vovelle in the week running up to 14 July, having instead made representations for a 'closed colloquium bringing together a score of historians of an identical viewpoint').

But for all his determination to rise to what he construed as the occasion, Vovelle himself had to confess that his task was predicated not simply on the certifiable 'malaise of the national community over the way to deal with this major moment of our collective memory', but more drastically on the memory of the Revolution being in the public mind 'very far along the road to extinction'. It was the depressing truth that, while the chattering classes continued to chatter in their inimitably brilliant Gallic way, the nation as a whole was paying very little attention. This was probably less a reflection of the fact that the Cold War was 'over', or because the emergence of the consensual republic had extinguished political passions, and more the outcome of the long history from 1880 onwards which, apart from times of crisis, had seen the divergence of state-sponsored commemoration and public holiday. But whatever the causes, it seemed a matter of incontestable fact that few outside the charmed circle of the metropolitan intelligentsia or the riven world of politicians jostling for position cared whether the true 'hero' of the Revolution was Mirabeau or Lafayette or Danton or Robespierre or the *sans-culottes*, whether the execution of Louis was justified regicide or brutal political murder, whether the Terror was imposed by 'circumstances' or wilfully generated by an insane political 'voluntarism', or whether the installation of 'Condorcet' in the Panthéon signified a rehabilitation of the

Girondins (an appropriately diplomatic veil drawn over the fact that the Girondins had been the more bellicose members of the war party). The issues that the historians, journalists and intellectuals had variously tried to keep alive were in the wider public imagination something of a dead letter.

In another of his speeches Mitterrand claimed that to 'remember' is to 'rejuvenate' or 'renew'. The one attempt at enacting this proposition with a degree of literalness came from an unusual quarter and in an unusual form. Someone at the Hôtel de Ville had the bright idea of bringing the Revolution back to 'life' by tracing living descendants of the original protagonists and arranging a reunion. Predictably enough, it turned out to be a somewhat lowering affair, degenerating fast into sulky and ill-tempered farce. A descendant of Robespierre, a right-wing journalist, disavowed his ancestor. Louis XVI's exceptionally distant kin refused to stand alongside the alleged posterity of his executioner, Henri Sanson. A relation of Danton, discovered in Peru, declared himself to be a man of the Right, while a descendant of Charlotte Corday insisted that she had not in fact been an assassin. So much for the spirit of fraternity. But if this was to take history a little too personally, at least the persons concerned took a view. Most of France had no view at all and for the most part in *la France profonde* the televised Goude show was greeted with a Gallic shrug. The Revolution was now more a *lieu d'oubli* than a *lieu de mémoire*.

At the time of the bicentennial *Le Nouvel Observateur* conducted a survey based on the question: what was the most important event of the French Revolution? The winning answer was 14 July and the taking of the Bastille. But pressed on what actually happened on the famous day, memory tended to draw a blank. Who, today, other than in some specialist corners of the academy, remembers Humbert, Cholat, Poupart, Hulin, Elie, Maillard et al.? Who indeed has ever heard of them? Perhaps this is simply Nature's way with History; forgetting is what comes naturally to us. In the meantime, the president's 14 July garden party remains a fixture, the *tout-Paris* version of the great and the good (the cost of Chirac's last estimated at nearly half a million euros of taxpayers' money a pop, a strange comment on what began as a dispute about representation and taxation). At first it was *le peuple*, real men on the ground, then that political abstraction *le Peuple*; now it is (the English term is the one used) 'people' in the sense of the celebrity culture, the beautiful people, those in the news, the denizens of what is now journalistically called the *république peopulaire*. On both left and right, earnest discourse on the republican virtue of secular 'equality' drones on, while turning a blind eye to the real challenges of 'integration' (altogether too expensive and, as some have put it, too 'divisive'). Instead, official talk of the republic one and indivisible focuses on the (non-) issue of headscarves (the bicentennial lip service to cultural 'difference' long forgotten). What, if anything and notwithstanding the 'multicultural' panache of the bicentennial, the immigrant communities of the contemporary *banlieue* make of what started in the old *faubourgs* is not hard to guess. Even Furet's eirenic view of the post-revolutionary settlement (as the republic of the centre) was to darken, as his eye wandered over the ravaged landscapes of the *banlieue*, where the liberal mantra of individual 'rights' had little meaningful purchase.

One of the organisations sponsoring the idea of the bicentennial was upliftingly called Vive 89. In ironic counterpoint, the most comprehensive study we have of the issues surrounding its reality – Steven Kaplan's brilliant book – bears, for the French edition, the more forlorn title *Adieu 89*. Not, it should be noted, *Au revoir* (although its author did point out, as germane to his own intention, that in some parts of France '*adieu*' can mean both '*bonjour*' and '*au revoir*'). Is it, then, farewell in the definitive sense *sub specie aeternitas*? Or was it Zhou Enlai who in fact got it right: it just *is* too early to tell? Even Quinet, who cast such a disabused gaze over the resources of memory, also wrote, in the same text: 'The dead are patient; let them wait.' In the meantime, as we also wait and in the interim ponder whether the bicentennial razz-matazz was more appropriately wrapped in Furet's shroud or draped in Goude's exotic costumery, perhaps it is best to think of it as a gigantic collage, dutifully headed by the trinity 'liberty, equality, fraternity', but captioned below in even larger type with the greeting 'Have a nice day' (the culturally dismal terminus of the spirit of the original *journée*). As a gesture to those whose taste in historical memory runs along sterner lines, there might also be a small corner in the collage reserved for Man Ray's provocative image, *Imaginary portrait of the Marquis de Sade*, which has the stormed Bastille in the background, all fire and smoke, and in the foreground a representation of the incandescent brain of the prisoner who wasn't there, the divine Marquis.

FURTHER READING

The literature of the storming of the Bastille and its more general background in the French Revolution as a whole is fittingly gigantic and irreducibly controversial. To list all the sources I have consulted, and others might theoretically consult, would be more a hindrance than a help. I have therefore opted for a minimalist further reading programme. The following bibliography confines itself to what I consider a curious reader, anxious to pursue these matters further, is likely to find most useful. Where the French sources are concerned, I have for the most part included works also available in English translation, though in connection with certain issues there is only the original French to hand.

For sheer narrative flair, nothing can beat the two historiographical classics of the nineteenth century: Jules Michelet's *Histoire de la Révolution française*, Paris, 1979 (*History of the French Revolution*, translated by Charles Cocks, edited by Gordon Wright, Chicago, 1967) and Thomas Carlyle's *The French Revolution: A History*, edited by K. J. Fielding and David Sorensen, Oxford, 1989. Both accounts are written from distinctive points of view, but have in common unsurpassed story-telling verve.

CHAPTER 1

Humbert's eyewitness report is included as an appendix in Jacques Godechot, *La Prise de la Bastille, 14 juillet 1789*, Paris, 1965 (*The Taking of the Bastille, 14 July 1789*, translated by Jean Stewart, London, 1970). Humbert's text is briefly discussed in the context of a more general survey of eyewitness testimony by Jules Flammermont, *La journée du 14 juillet 1789: fragment des mémoires inédits de L. G. Pitra, électeur de Paris 1789*, Paris, 1892. For those who wish to go straight to the sources, there is the admirable online service of the Gallica catalogue of the Bibliothèque Nationale. For contemporary press reports, see Jeremy D. Popkin, *Revolutionary News: The Press in France, 1789–1799*, Durham, NC, 1990.

CHAPTERS 2 AND 3

For an overview of the French Revolution and the antecedents of the storming of the Bastille, the following are recommended for clarity of exposition and masterful synthesis: J. M. Thompson, *The French Revolution*, Oxford, 1955; Georges Lefebvre, *La Révolution française*, Paris, 1957 (*The French Revolution*, translated by Elizabeth Moss Evans, London, 2004) and *Quatre-Vingt-Neuf*, Paris, 1939 (*The Coming of the French Revolution*, translated by R. R. Palmer, Princeton, 1989); Albert Soboul, *Précis d'histoire de la Révolution française*, Paris, 1962 (*The French Revolution, 1787–1799: From the Storming of the Bastille to Napoleon*, translated by Alan Forrest and Colin Jones, London, 1989) and *1789: l'an un de la liberté. Etude historique, textes originaux*, Paris, 1973; Claude Manceron, *Sang de la Bastille: du renvoi de Calonne au sursaut de Paris, 1787/1789*, Paris, 1987 (*Blood of the Bastille*, translated by Nancy Amphoux, New York, 1989); William

Doyle, *Origins of the French Revolution*, Oxford, 1999, and *The French Revolution: A Very Short Introduction*, Oxford, 2001; Rurt Scurr, *Fatal Purity: Robespierre and the French Revolution*, London, 2006. The reader should, however, be warned that the whole question of what 'caused' the French Revolution is a historiographical and ideological minefield. The 'classic' accounts emphasise the so-called 'nobles' revolt' and the defence of traditional privileges as a causal crux, leading to the convocation of the Estates-General and everything that then followed. On the other hand, the so-called 'revisionist' account either contests or modifies this 'monolithic' view, stressing the progressive erosion of Privilege in the course of the eighteenth century, along with the influential role of many of the more 'progressive' or 'enlightened' aristocrats. One unfortunate consequence of the more extreme versions of this approach is that it renders the outbreak of the Revolution effectively unintelligible.

CHAPTER 4

The most detailed and substantial scholarly account of the storming of the Bastille is Jacques Godechot's *The Taking of the Bastille*. Other studies include: Guy Chaussinand-Nogaret, *La Bastille est prise: la Révolution commence*, Paris, 1988 (exceptionally good on the relation between street violence and the evaporation of forms of political legitimacy and authority); Christopher Hibbert, *The Days of the French Revolution*, New York, 1980; Paul Chauvet, *1789: L'insurrection parisienne et la prise de la Bastille*, Paris, 1946. Simon Schama's *Citizens: a chronicle of the French Revolution* (London, 1989) tells the story of the storming at a cracking pace. On the history and literature of the Bastille prison, see Monique Cottret, *La Bastille à prendre: histoire et mythe de la forteresse royale*, Paris, 1986; Hans-Jurgen Lusebrink and Rolf Reinhardt, *The Bastille: A History of a Symbol of Despotism and Freedom* (translated by Norbert Schurer), Durham, NC, 1997. On the *Vainqueurs de la Bastille*, see Victor Fournel, *Les Hommes du 14 juillet: gardes françaises et Vainqueurs de la Bastille*, Paris, 1890; Joseph Durieux, *Les Vainqueurs de la Bastille*, Paris, 1911.

CHAPTERS 5, 6 AND 7

On the revolutionary festivals and related ceremonies, see Mona Ozouf, *La fête révolutionnaire, 1789–1799*, Paris, 1976 (*Festivals and the French Revolution*, translated by Alan Sheridan, Cambridge, Mass, 1991); Marie-Hélène Huet, 'Unsettled Memories. The Revolution Buries Its Dead', in Robert T. Denommé and Roland H. Simon (eds), *Unfinished Revolutions: Legacies of Upheaval in Modern French Culture*, Pennsylvania, 1998, pp. 121–37. On Bastille Day, see Rose-monde Sanson, *Les 14 Juillet (1789–1975): fête et conscience nationale*, Paris, 1976; Charles Rearick, *Pleasures of the Belle-Epoque: Entertainment and Festivity in Turn-of-the-Century France*, New Haven, 1985; Christian Amalvi, 'Le 14-Juillet. Du *Dies Irae* à *Jour de fête*', in Pierre Nora (ed.), *Les Lieux de mémoire*, Vol. I, *La République*, Paris, 1984, pp. 421–72. On the Centennial, see Pascal Ory, 'Le Centenaire de la Révolution française. La preuve par 89', ibid., pp. 523–60. On the Bicentennial, see Steven L. Kaplan, *Adieu 89*, Paris, 1993 (*Farewell, Revolution*, Vol. I, *Disputed Legacies*, Vol. II, *The Historians' Feud*, Ithaca, 1995, 1996; Jean-Noël Jeanneney, *La République a besoin d'histoire: interventions*, Paris, 2000; *Le Bicentenaire de la Révolution française: rapport du président de la Mission du Bicentenaire au président de la République sur les activités de cet organisme et les dimensions de la célébration*, Paris, 1990; David A. Bell, 'Liberté, Egalité, Have a Nice Day', *New Republic*, 23 January 1989.

On the general conceptual and political issues of 'interpreting' the French Revolution, see François Furet, *Penser la Révolution française*, Paris, 1978 (*Interpreting the French Revolution*, translated by Elborg Forster, Cambridge, 1981) and Eric Hobsbawm, *Echoes of the Marseillaise: Two Centuries Look Back on the French Revolution*, London, 1990. Their respective approaches are utterly different and provide the best available snapshot of just how riven the field is.

LIST OF ILLUSTRATIONS

1. Charles Thévenin, *Un Vainqueur de la Bastille*.
   Musée Carnavalet, Paris   2
2. Jean-Baptiste Lallemand, *La prise de la Bastille*.
   Musée Carnavalet, Paris   16
3. Isidore Helman after Charles Monnet, *The Opening
   of the Estates General*, 1790. Bibliothèque Nationale
   de France, Paris   38
4. French School (19th century), *The Storming of the
   Bastille, 14 July 1789*. Private Collection   62
5. Pierre-Antoine Demachy, *Fete de l'Unité, 10th August
   1793*. Musée Carnavalet, Paris   98
6. *La République sur la barque du Progrès*, engraving
   by Bellenger, in *L'Illustration*, 14 September 1889.
   Bibliothèque des arts décoratifs, Paris   128
7. Photograph of Jessye Norman singing the
   Marseillaise for the Bicentennial in the Place de la
   Concorde, Paris, 14 July 1989   158

ILLUSTRATION CREDITS

ACKNOWLEDGEMENTS

No one today (including those far better informed and more expert than myself) could, without suspicion of having been afflicted with a mild dose of insanity, seriously offer a short study of 14 July 1789 and its aftermath that claimed to embody a novel account or interpretation. In my own case, I can (if only in this respect) guarantee my sanity. For the most part the preceding pages are a digest or distillation (how competently executed will be for the experts to determine) of what others have written. Since the relevant literature is fittingly gigantic, I have relied for the most part on the historiographical 'classics': in the nineteenth century, Michelet, Carlyle and Tocqueville, with a company of outriders (for example, Burke and Taine); in the twentieth century, on some of the best-known of the 'professional' historians (a short list includes Lefebvre, Soboul, Thompson, Rudé, Cobb, Hobsbawm, Godechot, Furet, Ozouf). When I say 'rely,' I have to make clear that this is to be variously understood in relation to the different portions of this impressive archive. I rely on Michelet, Carlyle and (to a lesser extent, given the explicit terms of his own enterprise) Tocqueville, for a set of images and representations that inform a certain way of telling a story (or denying that there is in fact that much of a story to be told). This forms an important dimension of the story I myself try to tell. In the case of the twentieth-century historians (including very many not listed above), I rely on them in the more standard sense of going to them as sources of reliable information (although what they respectively do with this information is of course subject to often fiercely rivalrous interpretations of it). For my purposes, both corpuses are indispensable, with a strong trade-off element – broadly between flair and precision – as one shuttles between them.

At a more personal level, I have particular debts of gratitude to two specialist historians of the French Revolution, who also happen to be friends and colleagues: Ruth Scurr and Mike Sonnenscher. My heartfelt thanks to both. My most extended exchanges have been with my close friend Peter de Bolla (author of what is in many ways a companion volume in the Profile series, on 4 July and the American Revolution). He has been a constant intellectual companion, throwing out ideas and suggestions largely on the back of having read an earlier version of the manuscript. It is a source of regret for me that, for reasons of space, I was unable to take on board many of his fertile suggestions. But without his comments, the book as it is would not have been the same.

I dedicate the book to Clea, my ten-year-old daughter, who, I hope, may one day read it.

INDEX

A

Amont, Marcel 173
Antoinette, Marie 88, 102, 110
Argenson, René-Louis de Voyer, marquis de 58
Arné, Joseph 81, 87
Artois, Charles, comte de 47, 54, 152
Attali, Jacques 179
Aulard, Alphonse 161, 162, 181

B

Bailly, Jean Sylvain 86, 104, 117, 133
Balzac, Honoré de 63
Barnave, Antoine 51, 83
Baron 92
Barras, Paul 135
Barrès, Maurice 144, 148
Basch, Victor 144, 145, 150
Baudrillart, Henri 127

Bayet, Albert 151
Beaumarchais, Pierre 71
Bechade la Barthe, Jean 72
Beffroy de Reigny, Louis-Abel 90, 92
Bequart 80, 83
Besenval de Bronstatt, Pierre Victor 28, 66, 67, 73, 83
Bin, Emile 163
Blum, Léon 149, 151
Bonaparte, Napoléon 123, 124, 125, 133
Bonnemère, Aubin 75, 84, 90, 137
Boucheron, Pierre-Benjamin 77
Boulanger, Georges Ernest, général 166–7
Bourdon, Léonard (Bourdon de la Crosnière) 87, 90

Brienne, Loménie de 42, 43, 44, 45, 46, 48, 101
Brissot, Jacques-Pierre 70
Burke, Edmund 26, 31, 94, 113
Bush, George W. 34

C

Calonne, Charles Alexandre, vicomte de 40, 42, 43, 45
Carlyle, Thomas 18, 30, 35, 45, 91
Carnot, Lazare 160, 175
Carnot, Sadi 160, 162–3
Carra, Jean-Louis 100
Charles V 69
Charpentier, Marie 92
Chassin, Charles-Louis 160, 162
Chaunu, Pierre 31
Chéret, Jules 165
Chirac, Jacques 35, 167, 168, 177, 187
Cholat, Claude 81, 90, 187
Clair, René 149
Clemenceau, Georges 142
Clouet, Jean-François 84
Clovis 133
Condorcet, Marie Jean, marquis de 174, 176, 185

Corday, Charlotte 122, 153, 186
Corny, Ethis de 67, 77, 85
Coutan, Jules 164
Curtius, Philippe 101, 102, 107

D

Daladier, Edouard 151
Danton, Georges 51, 61, 64, 88, 89, 117, 118, 121, 162, 163, 185, 186
Darwin, Charles 165
Daumier, Honoré 142
Davanne 75, 84
David, Jacques-Louis 101, 102, 110, 180
De Gaulle, Charles 140, 154, 155
Deflue, Louis 85
Delacroix, Eugène 136
Delannoy, Aristide 142–3
Delavigne 76
Denain 75, 84
Dénot, François-Félix 81, 83, 86
Desmoulins, Camille 64, 65, 97, 102, 113, 121
Dickens, Charles 36
Diderot, Denis 64
Dreyfus, Alfred 140, 143–5, 146, 147, 150, 155, 159
Ducastel, Jean Baptiste 14

Duclos, Jacques 150
Dupin 14
Dusaulx, Jean-Joseph 90
Duverney, Paris, 72

E
Eglantine, Fabre de 142
Elie, Jacques-Job 8, 13, 79,
    80, 81, 82, 83, 87, 90, 91,
    187

F
Faguet, Emile 161
Fauchet, Claude abbé 76, 80
Faure, Edgar 174
Flesselles, Jacques de 7, 29,
    66, 82, 102
Foch, Ferdinand, maréchal
    148, 153
Foulon, Jean-François 29,
    30, 81, 82, 83, 86
Fouquier-Tinville, Antoine
    Quentin 102
Franklin, Benjamin 101
Fréron, Louis 87
Furet, François 179–85, 187,
    188
Fustel de Coulanges, Numa
    Denis 148

G
Gambetta, Léon 127

Gance, Abel 147
George III 21
Georget, Etienne, 14, 91
Giscard d'Estaing, Valéry
    169
Gochon, Clément 104
Godechot, Jacques 39
Goebbels, Joseph 153
Gorsas, Antoine-Louis 97
Grégoire, Henri, abbé 143,
    174, 175
Grévy, Jules 132
Grosholz, Marie (Mme
    Tussaud) 88, 101
Groslaire, Toussaint 91
Guéhenno, Jean 153
Guesde, Jules 141
Guignon, Louis 91

H
Hancock, John 23
Hébert, Jacques-René
    102
Hegel, Georg Wilhelm
    Friedrich 106
Hobsbawm, Eric 31
Hugo, Victor 125, 157
Hulin, Pierre-Augustin 8,
    79, 80, 81, 84, 87, 90, 187
Humbert, Jean-Baptiste,
    4–15, 24, 28, 83, 84, 87,
    187

J

Jackson, Michael 179
Jaurès, Jean 141, 144, 145
Jeanneney, Jean-Noël 174–5,
    176, 177, 178, 180
Jefferson, Thomas 22, 78
Joan of Arc 145
Joffre, Joseph, maréchal 148,
    153

K

Kaplan, Steven 188
Kropotkin, Peter 106, 115

L

La Corrège, Jean de 72
La Luzerne, César
    Guillaume de 60
La Salle, Adrien-Nicolas,
    marquis de 66, 89
Labarthe, Antoine 79
Lafargue, Paul 141
Lafayette, Marie-Joseph,
    marquis de 21, 28, 30, 47,
    82, 88, 89, 105, 107, 108,
    111, 112, 113, 117, 118,
    123, 133, 184
Lambesc, prince de 6, 65,
    66, 78
Lamoignon, Chrétien-
    François 44, 45, 46, 56,
    57, 88, 101

Lang, Jack 170, 171, 178
Larkin, Philip 18
Laroche, Bernard 72
Latude, Jean Henri 71, 100,
    103
Launay, Bernard-René de
    5, 8, 29, 68, 72, 73, 74, 75,
    76, 77, 79, 80, 81, 82, 83,
    84, 85, 87, 92, 102, 170
Lavabre, Guillaume 135
Laval, Pierre 154, 155
Lavallée, Eloi-Joachim 92
Lavigne, Raymond 141
Lebrun, Albert 151
Lefebvre, Georges 25, 152,
    181
Lefèvre, abbé 67
Liancourt, François
    Alexandre, duc de 30, 86
Linguet, Simon-Nicolas
    Henri 71
Losme, Salbrai de 82
Louis Philippe II (Philippe
    Egalité) 63
Louis XVI 5, 12, 21, 26, 29,
    43, 70, 71, 88, 102, 129, 186
Loustalot, Elysée 39, 99,
    113, 156

M

Mably, Gabriel Bonnot de
    88

Maillard, Stanislas 14, 80,
    81, 87, 90, 187
Marat, Jean-Paul 73, 93, 94,
    100, 102, 113, 114, 117,
    122, 153
Mariana, Juan de 135
Marmontel, Jean-François
    70
Martin, Henri 130–1
Mathiez, Albert 162, 181
Mazarin, Jules, cardinal
    69
Mercier, Louis-Sébastien 97,
    100, 105, 106, 108
Mercier, Benoît 91
Michelet, Jules 3, 14, 18, 31,
    32, 36, 71, 94
Mill, John Stuart 35
Mirabeau, Honoré Gabriel
    Riqueti, comte de 48, 50,
    55, 61, 71, 86, 88, 93, 103,
    111, 185
Mitterand, Danielle 175
Mitterand, François 167,
    168, 172, 174, 180, 186
Monet, Claude 134
Monge, Gaspard 175
Monnet, Jean 168
Morellet, André 70
Moussigny, Mlle 84
Mozart, Wolfgang
    Amadeus 156

N
Necker, Jacques 5, 41, 42,
    50, 52, 53, 54, 60, 64, 82,
    101, 102
Norman, Jessye 171, 172,
    173

O
Ormesson, Jean de 42, 47
Ozouf, Mona 181

P
Paine, Thomas, 4, 107
Palloy, Pierre-François 102,
    103, 104, 108, 111, 116,
    121
Pannetier, Jean-Armand
Parein Dumesnil, Pierre 88
Péguy, Charles 99
Pelletier, Laurent 92
Perrin, Antoine-Charles 92
Pétain, Philippe, maréchal
    148, 153 154, 155
Piquod de Sainte-Honorine
    77
Pouget, Emile 168
Poujade, Jean-Antoine 72
Poupart, Jean-Baptiste 64,
    77, 88, 187

Q
Quinet, Edgar 37, 182, 188

204 THE FOURTEENTH OF JULY

R

Raspail, Benjamin 129
Reubell, Jean 135
Réveillon, Jean-Baptiste 51,
    101
Richard, Jean Nicolas 14
Richelieu, Armand Jean
    Duplessis, cardinal 63,
    69
Richemont 79
Riefenstahl, Leni 178
Robespierre, Maximilien 17,
    29, 30, 33, 36, 44, 60, 61,
    74, 83, 87, 88, 102, 108,
    118, 119, 120, 123, 124,
    129, 146, 176, 177, 186
Rocard, Michel 171
Rochefort, Henri 129
Rolland, Romain 151
Rossignol, Jean 88
Rouget de Lisle, Claude
    Joseph 121, 171
Rousseau, Jean-Jacques
    101

S

Sade, Donatien Alphonse
    François, marquis de 71,
    72, 73, 188
Saint-Just, Louis de 36, 37,
    176
Sanson, Henri 186

Santerre, Antoine Joseph
    76, 87
Sarkozy, Nicolas 101
Sauvigny, Berthier de 82
Servan, Antoine 71
Sieyès, Emmanuel Joseph,
    abbé 48, 55, 124
Soboul, Albert 181
Solages, Hubert, comte de
    72
Sombreuil, marquis de 67
Souberbielle, Joseph 88
Soulès, Prosper 89

T

Taine, Hippolyte 32, 132,
    161
Talleyrand, Charles
    Maurice de 5, 107, 108,
    110
Tavernier, Jean-Baptiste 72
Thatcher, Margaret 167, 184
Thierry Augustin 148
Thuriot de la Rosière,
    Jacques-Alexis 74, 75, 76,
    85, 87, 90
Tocqueville, Alexis de 41,
    184
Tournay, Louis 75, 90, 92
Toussaint L'Ouverture,
    François-Dominique 146,
    175, 179

Turgot, Anne Robert
    Jacques 49, 50, 51, 52, 174

V
Vergennes, Charles Gravier
    de 12
Villette, Chales 104
Voltaire, François-Marie
    Arouet 70, 101, 104, 116
Vovelle, Michel 184–5

W
Wargnier, Louis Charles 79
Warhol, Andy 179
Whyte, James (Whyte de
    Malleville) 72
Wordsworth, William 115

Z
Zhou Enlai, 21, 35, 188

PROFILES IN HISTORY

Love affairs, battles, discoveries and rebellions have changed the course of world history. But some have turned out to be more significant than others: they have become icons in popular imagination, in drama, fiction and art; they have been argued and puzzled over, re-told and re-presented for centuries.

The *Profiles in History* series explores some of these iconic events and relationships of history. Each book starts from the historical moment: what happened? But each focuses too on the fascinating and often surprising after-life of the story concerned.

Profiles in History is under the general editorship of Mary Beard.

Published
Peter de Bolla: **The Fourth of July**
David Horspool: **Why Alfred Burned the Cakes**
Ian Patterson: **Guernica**
Clare Pettitt: **Dr Livingstone, I Presume?**
James Sharpe: **Remember Remember the Fifth of November**
Glyn Williams: **The Death of Captain Cook**
Emily Wilson: **Death of Socrates**
Greg Woolf: **Et Tu, Brute?**

Unpublished
Robert Irwin: **The Summer of '67**
Clair Wills: **Dublin 1916: The Siege of the GPO**

7/09